GOING PRO

The Deliberate Practice of Professionalism

Tony Kern

PYGMY BOOKS
Smaller. Smarter.

Colorado Springs, Colorado

A Pygmy Book
PUBLISHED BY PYGMY BOOKS, LLC

Going Pro: The Deliberate Practice of Professionalism
Copyright © 2011 by Tony Kern. All rights reserved.

Printed in the United States of America. No part of this book may be used or reproduced in any manner whatsoever without written permission except in the case of brief quotations embodied in critical articles and reviews. No part of this publication may be used, reproduced or distributed in any form or by any means, or stored in a data base or retrieval system, without the prior written permission of the publisher.

Pygmy Books takes environmental sustainability very seriously. We utilize print on demand publishing to conserve our natural resources, reduce overstocking, warehousing, and unnecessary waste while maintaining the highest standards of editorial review and quality. Additionally, we ship direct from printer to buyer to reduce the overall carbon footprint of our products.

This Pygmy Book is available at a discount for business, education, organizations, corporations and others interested in bulk purchasing.

For information please email:
Special Market Department, Pygmy Books, LLC,
pygmybooks@gmail.com

Cover & Book Design by Marcie Miller

ISBN 978-0-9842063-1-5

Information contained in this book has been obtained by Pygmy Books, LLC ("Pygmy Books") from sources believed to be reliable. However, neither Pygmy Books nor its authors guarantee the accuracy or completeness of any information published herein and neither Pygmy Books nor its authors shall be responsible for any errors, omissions, or damages arising out of use of this information.

This work is published with the understanding that Pygmy Books and its authors are supplying information, but are not attempting to render engineering or other professional services. If such services are required, the assistance of an appropriate professional should be sought.

Also From Tony Kern
Redefining Airmanship

Flight Discipline

Darker Shades of Blue: The Rogue Pilot

Controlling Pilot Error: Culture, Environment and CRM

Controlling Pilot Error: Approach and Landing

Blue Threat: Why to Error is Inhuman

Praise for Tony Kern's Previous Books
Redefining Airmanship

"This is an enthralling book about risk management on the flight deck. Anyone who needs to minimise risk in other professional situations will also find it helpful. Good energetic writing, lots of fascinating stories, makes managing risk exciting."
 – Dr. J. F. M. Oldham

"I am pretty sure that I can get by being a lousy fly caster and poor wing shot and still enjoy a pretty good life . . . I know that being anything other than an excellent pilot is unacceptable. Tony Kern has given us all a model to work with that is both comprehensive and systematic. He has illustrated it with clear real-life examples making each of the component concepts vivid. This book is a real treasure. It is at once a clear description of the destination and it is the map and the compass that we can all employ along on the way."
 – John Brietlinger, Minneapolis, Minnesota

"How important is this book? It is as important for pilots to read and re-read as Wolfgang Langewiesche's 'Stick & Rudder' . . . there is no higher praise. Dr. Kern proposes herein a simple but profound model to help us understand airmanship and he proceeds to support, explicate and instantiate that model using clear and well-chosen case material. This is good stuff!"
 – Frank Van Haste, Trumball, Connecticut

"Tony Kern has written a detailed, yet compelling, story for airmanship in the 21st century. His research is thorough, his examples are vivid, and his personal experience ties them together. As a safety professional, I was amazed to see that almost all of his 'lessons learned' could be applied to ground operations, as well as flight. Wish I'd written the book!"
 – Commercial Pilot, O'Fallon, Illinois

Flight Discipline

"This is certainly a must read book for pilots, from students like myself, to those on the top of the aviation food chain. Mr. Kern provides the WHY pilots MUST follow procedures like using checklists to making good decisions on when and when not to fly or the need to be in strict compliance. His points are illustrated with numerous mishaps and close calls when pilots chose to break the rules. There is nothing more riveting than to 'stand on the shoulder of giants' and learn from countless mistakes from both the military and civilian arenas of aviation. This most certainly will make me a better informed pilot. Thanks Lt. Col. Kern"
 – Richard Teves, Massachusetts

"Kern's Flight Discipline gives the reader an enormous education on professionalism in the cockpit in just under 400 pages. His book is one that should be on the required reading list for any serious pilot, especially those in crewed aircraft."
– Instructor pilot, Michigan

Darker Shades of Blue: The Rogue Pilot

"I am a commercial pilot and a physician. This book was introduced to me as a part of my recurring flight training. Ultimately, the themes made me redefine my medical practice as well. I have shared this book with dozens of people, pilots and non-pilots alike. Tony Kern has touched a fundamental theme by defining rogue behavior, including rogue behavior by individuals and by organizations. Fellow pilots understand the themes easily. Other people, including fellow physicians, have privately told me that they fundamentally changed their practice procedures as a result of reading this book. One non-pilot told me that I had "saved his life" by suggesting that he read this book. Contemplative people, involved in aviation or not, will do soul searching as a result of reading this book. Rogues will be angry (as could be expected from the basic tenants of rogue behavior). Almost all will recognize rogue tendencies in their own behavior and will confront a decision to make corrective actions or to continue. This is not a book with a lot of confusing technical jargon. I highly recommend that you read this book if you get a chance. I hope that demand will bring a new printing."
– Dr. Marvin Bowers, Tennessee

"Mr. Kern has succeeded in bringing to the forefront what I consider one of the greatest challenges to aviation: the rogue, undisciplined pilot. Rogues will continue to be a source of danger not only to themselves but their crews, passengers and people on the ground and this book should be required reading for everyone with a certificate (and even those who aren't pilots). Kudos to Mr. Kern for an eye-opening look at this threat."
– Seth Beckhardt, Port Orange, Florida

Blue Threat: Why to Err is Inhuman

"Throughout my toughest challenges as a reporter I've used *Blue Threat* both to do the work and work the problems. I've used the *Blue Threat* approach to do after assignment reviews to identify the fail points and the fixes. It's been vital in not only equipping me to deal with the demands of remote reporting, it's helped formulate a standard organisational approach to covering the island, and provided a framework for training and supporting other reporters."
– Andrew O'Connor, Television Journalist, ABC News, Perth, Australia

" ... this book is about identifying and dealing with the threats we pose to our own performance. But, don't worry. This isn't one of those touchy feely California Psycho-baloney books...What you will find mostly are tools to track your hazards and quantify your risks. Strategies for incremental (read, "painless") performance improvement are provided. This is an important book about an important topic, "Me." If you read it, and take just some of it to heart, it will make you better at what you do. No matter what that might be."
– Richard Keltner

Contents

	Acknowledgements	vii
	Introduction: Some Assembly Required	1
Chapter 1	The Case for Professionalism	21
Chapter 2	A Brief History of Professionalism	39
Chapter 3	Aren't We <u>All</u> Professionals?	63
Chapter 4	Setting the Bar: The New Professionalism	83
Chapter 5	The Deliberate Practice of Professionalism	105
Chapter 6	The Ethics of Professionalism	125
Chapter 7	Vocational Excellence: There is No Substitute for Talent	151
Chapter 8	Continuous improvement	175

Chapter 9	**Professional Engagement:** **Where the rubber Meets the Road**	199
Chapter 10	**Professional Image**	225
Chapter 11	**Selflessness**	249
Chapter 12	**Tying In the New Professionalism:** **Approaches that Work**	275
Chapter 13	**The Culture Connection:** **Building a Level III Organization**	293
	Appendix	312
	Selected Bibliography And Resources	319
	Index	324

Dedication

Joseph Kern III (1951-2011)

This book is dedicated to the memory of my brother, Joe Kern, who epitomized the personal and professional attributes of resiliency and selflessness better than any man I have ever known.

Acknowledgements

I haven't had an original thought in my life, and it is only though the collective insights, encouragement and prodding of others that this work came together.

I would specifically like to thank my beautiful wife Shari for her editing, insights, encouragement and patience. I am not an easy man to live with when I put my head down over a computer on a project of this magnitude.

Dan and Jodie Boedigheimer provided both ideas and grunt work on pre-reads, re-reads and made the book far better than it would have been without their insights.

Andrew O'Connor, my dear friend and fellow human performance zealot, provided not only insights and inspiration, but a key personal case study around which I was able to frame an entire chapter.

I want to thank everyone at Corvirtus, LLC for their assistance and insights on the difficult aspects of creating valid tools and assessments around the Level III concept.

I want to also thank NTSB Members Deborah Hersman, Robert Sumwalt, Chris Hart, Mark Rosekind, Earl Weener and all the staff at the National Transportation Safety Board for their invitation to keynote the 2010 Forum on Aviation Professionalism. It was this event, coupled with the continued support of Member Sumwalt and Dr. Evan Byrne that reminded me I had a project to finish. They were the key inspiration that drove this effort to completion.

Thanks to Marcie Miller for the layout and cover design, as well as her patience with the multiple "one more change" items that inevitably occur in my writing projects.

Finally, as always, I thank God for the gift of time and talents to give something back to the world that has given so much to me.

"You can spend your life any way you want to, but you can only spend it <u>once</u>."

Van Crouch, Author

Introduction

Some Assembly Required

"Slumber not in the tents of your fathers. The world is advancing. Advance with it."

Mazzini

INTRODUCTION 1

One of the universal truths in the world is that big things are made up of smaller things.

Whether we are talking about machines, furniture, organizational systems, or large human performance concepts such as *professionalism*, this universal truth holds. Because of their size and complexity, large things are unique in other ways as well. Typically, they come to us fully assembled or in parts with a schematic of the whole and instructions for assembly, operation and maintenance.

> "One of the universal truths in the world is that big things are made up of smaller things."

A box of parts without a picture of the whole and assembly instructions is not a "big thing in the making." It is a box of parts, and will likely remain so forever. Small things – not a big thing.

In point of fact, absent a picture of the whole and assembly instructions, a box of parts will likely result in lost or damaged pieces, or will be set aside for attempted assembly at some vague point in the future which never arrives. Or perhaps the owner, once optimistic about assembling and enjoying the big thing, becomes jaded and frustrated with the inability to assemble it and discards it forever. "If it was important" the big thing builder laments, "they would have given me a picture or at least provided me instructions. Maybe this isn't a big thing I need after all." Cynicism and apathy are often byproducts of this frustration.

> "Absent a picture of the whole and assembly instructions, a box of parts will likely result in lost or damaged pieces, or will be set aside for attempted assembly at some vague point in the future which never arrives."

There is a second critical aspect of this human performance conundrum. Not only is a lack of guidance a limiting factor, so is *time*. It takes time and effort to build big things. Every second of construction or delay builds relative momentum along a dynamic (growing) or entropic (decaying) performance curve of the future. If we are going to build a big thing, we need to get started – now – or at least very soon.

Professionalism is a big thing. A really big thing. It is vitally important, not only to each of us as individuals, but to our society as a whole. Although professionalism is a big thing with many moving parts, it is not overly complicated. As we will see in the pages that follow, *the deliberate practice of professionalism* will provide the design and assembly instructions, but relies on you to start putting the pieces together.

But before we go too far down that road, let's discuss the road we travelled to arrive at the content and structure of the new professionalism.

INTRODUCTION   3

A note on research process and methods

The research on professional standards actually began in 2003 when I started the heavy lifting for *Blue Threat*.[1] While researching an error control program for the United States Marine Corps aviation program, it became clear that there were a lot of differences of opinion regarding expected levels of professional performance for experienced personnel. I made a note to myself that if this were true *in the Marines*, it was likely far worse in the civilian world.

Now that my antennae were tuned for professionalism issues, I began to see episodes of unprofessionalism everywhere, many of which are highlighted in the following chapters. Analysis of these events led to the first cut of my research and resulted in a short list of "missing domains of professionalism." Then in May 2010, the National Transportation Safety Board held a three day international forum on *Professionalism in Aviation* in Washington DC. I was honored to be the keynote speaker at this event. Over those three days, it became clear a new set of standards of professionalism were needed, at least in aviation. A deep literature review was then conducted to find what other models of professionalism there might be to lean on, and I was surprised to find very little had been done in this area.

Over the next 15 months, a series of interviews, focus groups and surveys were conducted at various locations, all seeking to identify and quantify the core competencies of professionalism in modern business and government. In all, over 2,500 individuals were involved across a wide variety of industries and occupations. Further data reduction resulted in a comprehensive list of "professionalism

---

[1] Kern, Tony. *Blue Threat: Why to Err is Inhuman.* Pygmy Books. Colorado Springs. 2009.

behaviors" that were then clustered into six major areas - or *domains* of professionalism. As I applied these criteria to the real world, three general levels of professional emerged.

Level III professionalism

This book introduces the concept of *Level III professionalism*, the outcome of nearly three years of research into the nature of high performing professionals. The model continues to evolve, but at the time of this writing, includes the following six domains: *professional ethics, vocational excellence, continuous improvement, professional engagement, professional image,* and *selflessness*. Within these major areas there are 26 sub-domains and over 150 specific identified behaviors, all with developed metrics for assessment, training and observation.

The list is extensive, but not overly difficult to apply. While no one will become a Level III professional overnight, the application of the skills set forth in this book is a certain and very attainable path for anyone with a serious will to grow.

Let's take a quick look at the three levels, all of which are thoroughly discussed in chapter 4.

- Level I professionals are little more than *members* of a profession. They are competent enough to earn a paycheck, but not necessarily compliant with all the policies, procedures and regulatory guidance.
- Level II pros are also competent and are more ethically sound. They are referred to as *compliers*; they follow all the rules, but

never reach their full potential due in large part because there is no improvement process known or available to them. They tend to be *stagnant* professionals.

- Level III professionals embrace and continually improve across the six domains of professionalism. A Level III professional is known as a *professionalist*. The details associated with this elevated level of performance are fleshed out in more detail chapter 4.

Here is the integrated Going Pro model that illustrates the six domains and three levels of the new professionalism. You can readily see why we say that Level III professionals are "ten feet tall in a six foot world" of small or stagnant professionalism.

Going Pro Integrated Model of Professionalism

As an integrated model, these competencies are linked and cross referenced throughout the remainder of the book.

6   GOING PRO

Theoretical models are useful, but why would anyone who is currently getting by with the status quo put in the time or effort to achieve a higher level of professionalism?

Professionalism reignites the passion for excellence

To answer this important question, let's use a hypothetical example and consider the situation of a young lady named Josephine, who is five years into her career as a sales manager for *Widget Technologies*.

> Jo graduated in the top third of her class, majoring in business and was thrilled to land a job with *WidTech*. She received minimal training or professional development when she joined the team, but was told she should observe her colleagues closely and would "learn the ropes" through experience. What she observed was mediocrity.
>
> She made a few mistakes but was surprised when no one said much about it. "Everybody makes mistakes," she was told and pressed on, now comfortable with the cultural norms of average performance. She knew her mistakes had probably moved her off the fast track.
>
> Now and again, there was a bad outcome in her division. Someone would miss one too many quotas, or alienate a long time customer. When that happened, management would "hold someone accountable" and they were quietly moved aside or left the company. Jo learned from <u>this</u> experience, and became more risk averse. She wondered where the idealism and passion she once felt for her profession and company had gone. She started thinking about finding another job. She started

thinking about retirement, which was a long, long way off. She no longer enjoyed her job, but she needed it. She hunkered down to grind it out.

It is for people like Jo that the Blue Threat/Going Pro series is designed. There are thousands, perhaps millions of people like her out there; hard working, well meaning folks who would do better if they knew better. They want to grow. They want to achieve. They are long on passion (or at least once were), but short on resources and guidance. They want to reengage and discover the passion they once felt. They fly underneath the organizational radar, "grinding it out" day by day when all they need is a way to improve where they are, with the resources at hand, and a gentle nudge in that direction.

> "From a human capital perspective, the potential of this group of risk averse, underperforming 'B players' represents the largest untapped resource in the business world today."

From a human capital perspective, the potential of this group of risk averse, underperforming "B players" represents the largest untapped resource in the business world today.

The resources are now at hand for Jo and all those like her to (1) prevent the vast majority of self-inflected wounds accumulated through avoidable error; and (2) to grow into one's full potential as a professional.

The *Blue Threat* link

Although *Going Pro* can be read as a self-contained standalone work, this book is in fact the second in a two part series. The initial effort, *Blue Threat: Why to Err is Inhuman* (Pygmy Books, 2009) lays the foundation for personal responsibility and the "empowered accountability" approach, but with a focus on error control. The first words of *Blue Threat's* Chapter 1: *How Human Error Destroys Lives, Loves, Careers and Potential* sets the tone.

> Human error is the thief of human happiness and the slayer of dreams, careers, potential, and all too frequently – life itself. Viewing it as anything less hostile is to willfully expose your throat to the knife. Harsh words - intentionally so.
>
> For thousands of years, mankind has hidden behind Cicero's famous quote "to err is human." The cost is too great to continue on this apathetic and complacent path. So we are going to change the dialog. To *improve* is human, to *grow* is human, to *learn* is human. But to persevere in avoidable error at great risk to our lives, family, friends and careers – that is <u>in</u>human. It is time for some new poetry on this subject.
>
> Unintentional and avoidable errors end lives, poisons relationships, squanders wealth, feeds addictions, and ruins careers. It has ever been so. Error is a persistent and progressive thief, who will continue to steal from you and your potential as a human being on an ever greater scale until you make a conscious decision to stop being a passive victim.[2]

With this empowered accountability approach established toward error control, we now turn our attention to "going pro," becoming all we are capable of as professionals in this book.

The major difference between the two books is the focus of improvement. *Blue Threat* challenges the "to err is human"

---

[2] Kern, Tony *Blue Threat: Why to Error is Inhuman*, p. 13-14

argument and laser targets personal error control. By removing the "flawed species" excuse, it sets the stage for this professionalism discussion and personal growth. After all, it's hard to be a world class professional when you are still leaking high performance from controllable, self-inflicted wounds. But once those wounds are patched and the personal improvement process is moving forward, we must keep the ball rolling.

Going Pro takes the logical next step in the process by leveraging the same personal feedback principles to accelerate growth towards a set of specific skills that have been identified as the core elements of best-in-class professionalism. The relationship is illustrated in the figure below.

Level III performance. Stop the self-sabotage of preventable errors, and then maximize learning, growth and professionalism to reach your highest potential.

Both books rely on a common framework of objective self-awareness and a process of personal feedback based upon defined standards. The two books are also aligned in that they both target the top of the class – existing or potential high achievers. The underlying prerequisite for a self-improvement approach to work is the will of the individual. These books are written for people and organizations who *want* to get better, a group perhaps distinct from those who *need* to.

Be that as it may, this approach is also a key accelerator for personal and organizational culture change regardless of their current

"The underlying prerequisite for a self-improvement approach to work is the will of the individual. These books are written for people and organizations who *want* to get better, a group perhaps distinct from those who *need* to."

level of performance. Even in low performing organizations, a few high performing individuals are often the key to setting new standards and tipping the scale towards a positive and predictable culture shift. Level III professionals have a dramatic ripple effect.

From the organizational systems perspective, the tools and techniques offered in the Blue Threat/Going Pro series are potentially of even greater benefit. Developing a cadre of Level III professionals can act as both a catalyst for change and as an anchor point for realizing the values, vision and strategy of the organizational leadership across traditional functional lines. This "inside-out culture change" aspect is explained in detail in chapter 13.

The reciprocal nature of professionalism and error control

Although Going Pro builds progressively on the Blue Threat model, there is also a reciprocal benefit. Armed with new insights and tools for reaching Level III performance, professionals are able to see and avoid far more error producing conditions. This concept is illustrated in the following figure.

INTRODUCTION 11

Error control is enhanced as professionalism increases.

This makes sense in that *professional ethics, continuous improvement* and *professional engagement* all lend themselves nicely to the identification and remediation of error precursors.

Because the two works are so closely related on many topics, the books are linked by necessity. I quote frequently from *Blue Threat* inside these covers in order to establish and strengthen both bookends of error control and professional growth. In the end, my intent was to have a single philosophical framework with a practical set of skills and tools common to both error control and professional growth, ready for immediate application. In this regard, I hope I have not failed the reader.

Overview

As you read the pages that follow, you will see that holistic professionalism is indeed a very big thing made of many small parts. Yet they are definable parts, learnable parts, and measurable parts. Most importantly, they are connectable and actionable by individuals without specialized expertise in any specific area. It is important to state from the outset that it is not the intent of this book to be the final word on anything, but rather to provide clear and actionable steps for personal and organizational improvement and stimulate discussion on this critical topic of professionalism.

Each area we delve into has its own specialized experts, many of whom will likely take exception to the elements from their cherished fields that I have chosen to include, as well as those I have neglected. That is the burden of all synthesizers and integrators and I neither shirk from the task nor apologize for my inclusions or exceptions. Throughout, I attempt to provide the reader with footnotes and recommendations for deeper study from those with greater depth in specific fields than I am able to offer.

The organization of the book is designed around two goals, *understanding* and *improvement*.

Organization and format

As I began this pursuit of a new perspective on professionalism, it became clear from the onset that there are a lot of assumptions and opinions around, but very few facts or definitions. Therefore my first task was to provide some structure around which to have a rational discussion of the topic. Those impatient for specific action steps will likely find the first few chapters tedious, but I felt it critical to lay out the rationale and history surrounding the topic. Those who are merely looking to understand the topic from an academic perspective will likely find parts of the middle chapters a bit too mechanical and vocational. The dual objectives of *understanding* and *improvement* drove the organization and sequence of the chapters that follow. Here is a quick overview for those who like to gouge the introduction before making a buy decision.

We begin in chapter 1, *The Case for Professionalism*, with a look at the significance of the problem of poor professionalism in modern business and government. We discover that in an electronically linked world, single acts of unprofessional behavior can have devastating consequences for an individual, organization or industry.

In chapter 2, *A Brief History of Professionalism*, we look through the long lens of history to see how we arrived at our current state of affairs. This detailed explanation of cause and effect may be extraneous for some readers who come only looking for the tools. If this is you, I assure you I won't be offended if you decide to skip this chapter for the time being. As an historian, I feel it is important to understand the problem of apathy and *laissez faire professionalism* is rooted in our deep past. Some of our solutions may come from there as well.

Chapter 3, *Aren't We All Professionals?*, begins to rough in the structure of the new professionalism and starts by asking the rhetorical question from the chapter title. You may be surprised by the answer. Three levels of professionalism are defined and the goal of becoming a Level III professional – a *professionalist* – is established.

In chapter 4, *Setting the Bar: The New Professionalism*, we continue with deeper definitions and begin to outline specific standards, weights and measures to bring the previously fuzzy ideal of professionalism into sharper focus. Six weighted *domains of professionalism* are introduced along with their relative importance to the overall professionalism equation.

Chapter 5, *The Deliberate Practice of Professionalism* dives deep into the research on how world class experts are developed. The proven, but difficult, practice of *deliberate practice* is explained and eight steps for implementing the discipline are described in enough detail to get you started.

In chapter 6, *The Ethics of Professionalism,* we begin the deep dive into the first of the six domains of professionalism and deal forthrightly with the ethical demands of true professionals. We point out the dangers of so called *situational ethics* and illustrate how easy it is for even well meaning professionals to fall into rationalizations for unethical acts. Using the Atlanta Public Schools cheating scandal as a case study, we illustrate how organizations can fall hard if their priorities get confused.

Chapter 7, *Vocational Excellence: There is No Substitute for Talent,* brings us to the topic of job skills. After dealing with the important question of where to find standards for your particular vocation, we move into the key to developing professionalism standards with a deep set of *roadblocks, on ramps,* and *fast lanes* to assess and guide your vocational improvement efforts toward Level III standards.

Continuous improvement is the topic in chapter 8, and in this chapter we place the burden of improvement squarely on the shoulders of every would-be Level III professional. Improvement strategies are outlined and specific tools are provided for this vital component of growth-based professionalism.

Chapter 9, *Professional Engagement: Where the Rubber Meets the Road*, tackles the challenge of how to put your new skills into play through engagement with others. A detailed section on the lost art of *customer service* provides an expanded definition of the concept with applications for the daily work environment. A self-assessment and comprehensive list of immediate action steps conclude the chapter.

In chapter 10, we take *Professional Image* concerns to task, pointing out that image goes well beyond physical appearance. All aspects of interpersonal contact are discussed including a detailed look at the emerging image issues surrounding social media websites. The emphasis on crafting the *reality* rather than the image of professionalism is stressed throughout.

We conclude the six domains of the new professionalism with chapter 11, *Selflessness*. We kick off this chapter with the oxymoron that selflessness is in your best interest if professional growth is your goal. Discussions and tools for active listening, ego control, and mentorship are cornerstones of this chapter.

Chapter 12, *Tying In the New Professionalism: Approaches that Work* is all about integration. Four human performance concepts are analyzed with an eye towards seamlessly integrating standards of the new professionalism into the tapestry of organizational performance with technology, systems and other performance enhancing drivers. We conclude the chapter with a discussion on the limits of self-reliance as a prelude for our final chapter.

Chapter 13 concludes our journey and brings the challenge of elevating professionalism inside an entire organization with *The*

Culture Connection: Building a Level III Organization. The "crystal model" of bottom up culture change is introduced and specific options for implementation are brought to the table.

A note on style

As you may have already noticed, I write in the first person, not because I consider myself to be an authority on any given subject, but simply because I communicate best in this manner. On occasion, I share personal "war stories" and one or two irreverent observations. I believe a good book is a dialog between the writer and the reader. For this author, a personal communication style is my best effort in this regard.

Summary

This is a book about human performance – yours and your organization's. Perhaps you can already feel your self-defense mechanisms kicking in. "What business is it of this guy to question my professionalism? He doesn't know anything about me or my company. He doesn't know what I do, who I work for. He has never even met me." Those feelings are natural, and good. It shows you care. That is the essential starting point.

There is a general malaise in western society regarding the relative importance of professionalism. We often feel that our contributions and ideas are lost in the vastness of large systems, long term programs or corporate or government bureaucracies. It often seems that the only time our performance is recognized is when we fail. This malaise is a quicksand bog from which we must quickly escape. Only then we can chart our path and build our future.

So, let's get started and build a GREAT BIG THING together, a personal and occupational culture of professionalism that sweeps the infection of apathy and sloppiness from our industries and society.

The change starts now, and it begins with you.

"What worries me is the professionalism of everything."

Irvine Welsh, Author and Playwright

Chapter 1

The Case for Professionalism

"And whatever you do, do it heartily, as to the Lord and not to men."

Colossians 3:23

THE CASE FOR PROFESSIONALISM

As I sipped my first coffee at the local Starbucks, a young twenty something moved in a clockwise circuit around the coffee house, wiping down the dark walnut stained furniture with some type of pleasantly scented cleaning solution. Apparently, she was not yet a fully certified *Barista* and had been relegated the unenviable task of ensuring the tables, chairs, and loungers that made up the prototypical Starbucks interior were ready for the morning commuter rush. My Omega *Speedmaster* read 6:01 AM.

As an early riser with the oft associated coffee addiction, I had seen this routine many times before, usually done haphazardly in a few minutes by someone whose lack of enthusiasm for the task was indicated in the smears and streaks left behind on the tables and chairs. The evidence wouldn't become visible until around 6:30 (this time of year) when the sun spilled in through the east facing windows onto the table tops to reveal the shoddy work.

But there would be no streaks or smears today. As I observed the young lady at her task, she was clearly *serious* about making sure everything was cleaned and shined. Every corner on every table, every leg of every chair, the folds and creases in each leather lounger—she meticulously went over with the cleaning solution, then water, and finally a third dry rag. I was somewhat taken back by this attention to detail and level of diligence, the likes of which I had not seen since the days when I observed USAF Academy cadets preparing for white glove room inspections. Even against *those* standards, what I was witnessing was exceptional performance.

As she reached my table, I told her I appreciated her good work and asked if Starbucks had instituted a new quality assurance or training initiative that required the rigor of the "three rag" system, or perhaps if someone from corporate headquarters was visiting today. While I had been surprised by what I had seen so far, what she said next completely blew me away.

"No, nothing like that," she explained simply; *"I just like to do a good job, it's the way my parents raised me."*

In that simple sentence, the essence of the revival of American professional excellence was contained. Unfortunately, not everyone is taught that doing a good job has its own rewards.

We are off to a bad start in the new millennium. Over the past decade, we've heard a lot about a lack of professionalism in all sectors of industry and government. A few examples include:

- High end financial types spinning Ponzi schemes or taking on huge financial risks for their clients without any personal risk or remorse due to their golden parachute contracts.
- Surgeons operating on the wrong patient, the wrong part of the right patient, or simply botching the effort so badly that it kills or maims their patient.

- Professional pilots drunk in the cockpit, mistakenly landing on taxiways, and overflying destinations while playing with their laptop computers.
- Air traffic controllers bringing a blanket and pillow to work so they can take a nap during slow traffic periods.
- Clergy who abuse their positions of trust and authority to take advantage of their parishioners, both physically and financially.
- Police officers who take bribes or extort money or other favors from those they are sworn to serve and protect.
- Politicians who … well there aren't enough pages in this book to cover *that* list.

All of these gross and unseemly acts have three things in common.

- First, they are incongruent with the norms and standards of their profession.
- Second, they rise to the level of "newsworthiness" that attracts the interest of a researcher or reporter to write about them and put them in the public eye.
- Third, they all mask the *real* problem we face.

These high visibility acts are just the tip of a much larger iceberg; one that puts our entire Republic at significant risk. Unprofessional attitudes and behaviors run much deeper than the corruption and extreme malfeasance illustrated in the cases above. It is a far more insidious, subtle, and dangerous adversary. And the clock is ticking to address the challenge, especially in high risk industries like aviation, which are about to experience a dramatic shift in demographics due to an out of balance, aging workforce. Many industries and organizations are in similar situations as the baby boomer generation heads for the golf course.

The mathematics of unprofessionalism

Based upon the simple mathematics of exposure, the real problem of unprofessional behavior is not the one-off events that make the news. It's not the drunk pilot in the cockpit, the Ponzi-scheming financier, the surgeon who cuts off the wrong leg, or the child molesting clergyman. It's the cashier who is rude to a first-time customer who will never return to your store, the abrasive driver's license clerk who stokes anti-government resentment with his consistently negative attitude day in and day out, or the customer care representative who doesn't promptly return phone calls and drives previously loyal customers to the competition. It is the teacher who has lost interest in her students' learning, the burnt out businessman who no longer gives a damn about profit and loss, and the auto mechanic who uses second hand parts out of convenience. If we stop to think, and play each of these scenarios out over the hundreds of lives touched by each of these individuals, what you come up with is a true equation for the staggering costs of unprofessional behavior in our society.

Millions in moments

Unprofessional behaviors and attitudes act as fulcrums of opinion that leverage entire systems. When a professional business traveler encounters a rude gate agent who won't look up from her computer screen to help him change a middle seat to an exit row, they often form an opinion about an airline, not an individual. Whether this is fair or not to the airline doesn't really matter. As business travelers often do, this individual will likely share the negative story many times over with fellow business travelers, who may then search their memories for similar negative anecdotes about that particular company, as in "Oh yeah, if you think that is rude behavior, let me tell you about the time when . . ."

In fact, many people will actively and intentionally go out of their way to share a negative story as often as possible as a means of personal retribution against a company who would allow such behavior by their employees. In the era of social media where a single individual can literally reach millions in moments, this is a very real concern, as the following example illustrates.

Steve Dorfman is the Founder and CEO of *Driven to Excel*, a consulting firm specializing in aligning professional behavior with a corporate mission. His blog, *D2E*, is read by thousands. In February, 2009, Steve posted this story about a single episode he encountered while traveling.

> *We stood there, dumbfounded* ... while attempting to make an airline connection ... my girlfriend (Maggie) and I took our paper tickets to the counter to get our seat assignments. As we approached the desk, the clerk, "Mariana" had her head down and was carrying on about her weekend to the person on the other end of the phone. When she finally looked up, we were greeted with a half-smile (no words—she still had the phone held against her ear). For the next 31 minutes (we timed it), Mariana continued with her personal phone conversation and occasionally pecked at the computer keyboard, never really telling us what she was doing. Maggie and I just kept looking at each other, as if to say, "I can't believe this is actually happening." We felt like we were interrupting her personal life. We had been led to believe that she *could* help us with a situation stemming from an overcharge. As it turns out, she couldn't and we only ended up at another desk with more "can't do-ers."

In this manner, single unprofessional acts cascade as *negative force multipliers* into the system with the strong possibility of an exponential impact. And most of the time, no one in the host organization leadership hierarchy will ever know where it started.

The real magnitude of the professionalism black hole is best measured not by the newsworthy actions of a few true outliers who have a major impact on a few people. Rather, to turn the tide we must focus on the multitudes who continue to "functionally malfunction" beneath the radar, subtly and negatively impacting multiple people and situations day in and day out. While we have some indicators of the size of this problem, such as the $37 *billion* dollar loss estimate from the banking industry due simply to people not knowing what their jobs were,[1] we are left to merely guess at the true costs of unprofessionalism, or the gains that might be made by activating the untapped professionalism of compliant but disengaged workers who would willingly "do better if they knew better."

Culture clubs: Boiling frogs think they are fine

One reason we don't see or hear as much on the topic of poor professionalism as we should is that the vast majority of us have simply acclimated ourselves to it and lowered our expectations. Much like the proverbial frog who will calmly lie in water that is heated to the boiling point, we do not recognize the change in temperature until it is too late for us to do much about it. With

---

[1] *Executive Summary. $37 Billion: Counting the costs of employee misunderstanding.* White paper found at www.cognisco.com/downloads/white-paper/uk_exec_summary.pdf

regards to professional standards and behaviors, this is commonly discussed under the banner of *culture*, a topic we devote an entire chapter to later in this book.

Once cultural norms of behavior have set in, they can be difficult to notice, more difficult to accept, and often nearly impossible to change, especially from the inside of the organization or culture itself. This is true because as a member of a so-called profession, one is naturally resistant to both criticism and calls for change from perceived "outsiders" (like me). Psychologist Dietrich Dörner, the Director of the Cognitive Anthropology Project at the Max Plank Institute in Berlin and the author of *The Logic of Failure*, explains why those closest to a problem have the most difficulty recognizing and correcting it.

> The ability to admit ignorance or mistaken assumptions is indeed a sign of wisdom, and most individuals in the thick of complex situations (or professions) are not, or not yet, wise. People desire security ... and this desire prevents them from fully accepting the possibility that their assumptions may be wrong or incomplete.[2]

Often, this "lack of wisdom" about a particular culture in which we operate has a darker side. The natural reaction from many inside an industry to reports of unprofessional behavior or calls for greater professionalism is to (1) deny the problem, (2) band together in a defensive posture, and (3) attack the messenger. Time and again we have seen this play out to the detriment of all involved.

This cultural dynamic sets up a situation where challenging the status quo from the inside puts one at risk of ridicule and ostracism

---

[2] Dörner, Dietrich. *The Logic of Failure: Recognizing and Avoiding Error in Complex Systems*. Perseus Books. Cambridge Massachusetts, 1996. p. 42.

from your professional colleagues and peers, and challenging it from the outside is an invitation to personal and professional attacks from the industry gatekeepers and spin doctors.

In light of this reality, where can we turn to gain leverage on a decaying professional culture? The answer is closer than you can imagine. The problems might be societal, but the solutions can—and perhaps must—ultimately be personal.

The personal side of the professionalism gap

There is no question that individuals who work in industries or companies that tacitly allow unprofessional behaviors are impacted personally. A company that does not perform to expectations will eventually lose business as their customers vote with their feet and their wallets. Layoffs, loss of benefits, or simply the inability to advance in one's chosen profession is often the result of poor professionalism by a few, which damages the reputation of all.

Yet, as problematic as the cultural, governmental, and societal barriers are, **individuals and organizations remain uniquely empowered to perform to higher professional standards, and in so doing, create a peer-to-peer positive force for change.** As simple as this effort sounds, there are a few tough challenges to overcome, the first being the ability to see the need for change when we look in the mirror.

Again, Dörner helps us understand the underlying problem.

> An individual's reality model can be right or wrong; complete or incomplete. As a rule it will be both incomplete and wrong, and one would do well to keep that probability in mind.[3]

So, the first question we should ask is not, *am I a part of a professional industry or organization?*, but rather, *am I behaving professionally within it?* This is the most critical first step on the path to becoming ten feet tall in a six foot world. Yet even with this realization, this will not be an easy task for most.

Questions of personal and organizational behavior relating to professionalism tug hard at our self-esteem, which in modern society is a political correctness no-no of the highest order. This need not be so.

Note the present tense of the question, *am I behaving professionally?* This is not an attack on someone's overall professional stature; it is merely a question about current behavior. In point of fact, simply asking the question, *am I behaving professionally?* of oneself is an indicator that your personal or organizational professionalism "give a damn" needle is at least capable of coming off the wall and that you are fully capable of confronting the self-deception challenge that Dörner describes in the quote above.

Now armed with the vital question and the courage to ask it, the next challenge is how to find an accurate answer.

---

[3] Dörner, Dietrich. *The Logic of Failure: Recognizing and Avoiding Error in Complex Systems.* Perseus Books. Cambridge Massachusetts, 1996. p. 42.

Compared to what?

In spite of the serious and far reaching nature of the problem of poor professionalism, it is difficult to fault anyone for being inept at something that has never been clearly defined, let alone trained or formally evaluated. As a society, organization, or individual, we may have an *expectation* of professionalism, but without a *standard* we are reduced to a hint, hype, and hope methodology fueled by little more than lofty rhetoric from executives and ever more frequent "calls to action" from other stakeholders when their vague expectations are not met.

The way we never were

We haven't lost our professional way; we may have never known it, at least not collectively. This may seem difficult to accept for those whom a set of core principles of professionalism were provided at some point in their lives by their parents, coaches, scoutmasters, or others. But the evidence suggests that this "common understanding" is becoming less the norm than the exception, and frequently leads to a nostalgic approach often referred to as "back to basics."

In one example of rose colored hindsight, Federal Aviation Administration (FAA) Administrator Randy Babbitt said in 2010 "there is an extreme need to *refocus* (emphasis added) on professionalism" citing the "sad example" of the airline flight crew who "lost total situational awareness" and overflew their intended destination by hundreds of miles with an airliner full of passengers. "I can't regulate professionalism," he lamented. The problem with Administrator Babbitt's statement is that we can never re*focus* on the topic of professionalism since it has been blurry from the beginning. Even if it seems as if things are getting worse, there is no "back to the future" pathway available on the topic of professional behavior. We must design and create the future we desire.

> "There is no 'back to the future' pathway available on the topic of professional behavior. We must design and create the future we desire."

So rather than framing the challenge we face as a matter of correcting unprofessional behaviors, a more useful model might be to determine how to bring out the untapped and untrained professionalism in each of us. This returns us to the nub of the issue—what exactly are we talking about when we speak of *professionalism*?

Terms and definitions matter

Professionalism seems like a fairly straight forward, commonly understood term, but it has proven to be anything but. When we are dealing with something as critical and potentially inflammatory as professionalism, words do matter. This was illustrated in May 2010 at the National Transportation Board (NTSB) forum on *Professionalism in Aviation*, where I was honored to be the keynote speaker. In her introductory remarks, NTSB Chairman Deborah Hersman said:

> So many in the industry recognize this issue of professionalism is a real challenge … how do you encourage people day in and day out to do the right thing every time when people aren't watching?[4]

Over 50 industry experts wrestled with this challenge for three days without coming to any significant conclusions or even a shared definition of the concept or the level of problem it posed. Many at the event even argued that the very concept of public discussion of the topic put the industry in a bad light in the eyes of the public and, therefore, was ill-advised. The one significant insight was that if the aviation industry wanted to make any real progress on the issue of professionalism, we had some work to do. The aviation industry is certainly not alone is this regard.

Dark matter

Professionalism seems to be something that is best recognized—at least for now—by its absence, and that is a major part of our current challenge. It seems the only time we really hear anything about the topic is when it reaches the level of performance where one can't ignore it any longer; therefore, beginning to understand the true nature of this elusive concept might best begin by looking at what professionalism isn't.

Let's define some of the negative space by looking at a legal definition of *unprofessional*.

---

[4] Personal notes. NTSB Professionalism in Aviation Forum. May 18, 2010.

THE CASE FOR PROFESSIONALISM

unprofessional *adjective;* amateurish, contrary to professional ethics, improper, imprudent, inappropriate, injudicious, nonexpert, not of high standards, unbusinesslike, undignified, unethical, unfitting, unscholarly, unseemly, unsuitable for the culture or profession[5]

From this definition we see several elements emerge that are perhaps helpful, including *ethics, expertise, judgment, knowledge,* and *appearance,* among others. But can something as vital as professionalism be allowed to be defined merely by the absence of its negative? The answer to this question is far more than semantics because it deals with the critical issues of resources, attention, and priorities. If we do not choose to make the pursuit of professionalism separate from the frequency of its antithesis, we are unwittingly committing to a reactive, start and stop process driven by the behaviors of our least professional cadre. **That doesn't seem to make sense, because even if we experience a prolonged absence of unprofessional acts, we get no closer to the pot of gold that is *professionalism*.**

> "If we do not choose to make the pursuit of professionalism separate from the frequency of its antithesis, we are unwittingly committing to a reactive, start and stop process driven by the behaviors of our least professional cadre."

Let's begin this search for higher ground with a shared sense of humility. It seems clear from even a casual analysis of the topic that there is a lot we do not yet know.

---

[5] Burton's Legal Thesaurus, The McGraw-Hill Companies, Inc., 2007

Chemist and philosopher of science Michael Polanyi framed the humble approach to discovery nicely when he wrote:

> The process of discovery begins when we observe, often vaguely, a gap between what is and what could be. Our intuition tells us something better is just beyond the range of our mind's eye. To build a culture of discovery, we must encourage, not discourage, the passionate pursuit of our own and other's hunches.[6]

The core purpose of this book is to outline and promote a few well thought out "hunches" about professionalism, the first being that no one has cornered the market on its secrets just yet. There does not seem to be a "professionalism guru." Most of us have a feeling that "we know it when we see it," and most everyone readily recognizes when it is not there.

To frame this first global effort on the nature of professionalism, I'd like to suggest a comparison from the hard sciences, where NASA scientists tell us the limits of what they know about our universe. They look for something they know is there, but cannot yet clearly see or define.

> More is unknown than is known. We know how much dark energy there is because we know how it affects the Universe's expansion. Other than that, it is a complete mystery. But it is an important mystery. It turns out that roughly 70% of the Universe is dark energy. Dark matter makes up about 25%. The rest—everything on Earth, everything ever observed with all of our instruments, all normal matter—adds up to less than 5% of the Universe.[7]

---

[6] Polanyi, Michael. The Tacit Dimension. University of Chicago Press. 2009
[7] http://science.nasa.gov/astrophysics/focus-areas/what-is-dark-energy/

So let me get this straight. With all our science and technology and advanced computational power, we can't even observe 95% of the known universe we call outer space, and we are still struggling to explain the other 5%? That is a little frightening, and seriously humbling, which makes it a good metaphor and starting point for a useful conversation on the unknowns of "inner space" relating to this thing we call *professionalism*.

In this effort, it will not be enough to merely define professionalism by its presence or its absence. If it is important at all, we must be able to discriminate at deeper levels to create trainable, measurable, and observable knowledge, attitudes, skills, and behaviors. The purpose of the new professionalism initiative is to ignite the effort for dramatically enhanced professional competencies and to reach out to those for whom professionalism is a passion.

The hour of change is upon us.

It is well past professional midnight and time for everyone who calls themselves a "professional" to look in the mirror, and then each other in the eye, and demand that we adhere to the new set of shared standards.

Let's begin our journey with a couple of questions about our collective past. Where did this idea of professionalism come from? Has it always been a soft target?

> "The word career is a divisive word ... that divides the normal life from professional life."

Grace Paley, American Writer

Chapter 2

A Brief History of Professionalism

"A small body of determined spirits fired by an unquenchable faith in their mission can alter the course of history."

Mohandas Gandhi

Words are important, and the word *professionalism* might just be the most important word in 21st century business and government.

This chapter is about the evolution of the concept and term *professionalism*. For some readers who come to this book looking for "the gouge" on the new professionalism, this historical sojourn may seem to be an unnecessary sidetrack. If you are among these, feel free to skip forward to chapter 3, where we will pick back up the scent of the new professionalism. As an historian, I think it important that we comprehend how we got to the problems we have today. I realize we live in a drive-thru, microwave, give-it-to-me-quick world, but some problems are best understood through the long lens of history.

When it comes to understanding why professionalism has become controversial in many modern industries, words are more than mere semantics.

Anthropologically speaking, language is the principle factor that separates us from Chimpanzees,[1] with whom we apparently share 96% of our genes.[2] The one thing that allows us to stand on the outside of the zoo cage—at least for now—is our ability to use language to store and share knowledge. Yet, as critical as language is to our species, we treat this amazing gift with casual disdain, or worse, intentionally misuse words to deceive or manipulate each other.

Words allow us to transfer information and ideas from one person to another and, perhaps more importantly, from one generation to another. Words form the foundation of all learning beyond our direct experience. My philosophy professor at Albion College once explained that words are not designed by linguists in Noah Webster's laboratory for a specific purpose; they evolve through use by people in the real world. This use may be casual, or very intentional and manipulative, and the result is often a new word, or more often a new interpretation of an old word. He then made his key point, that language is a very powerful and living thing. Words mean things, and people skilled in the use of language—verbal or written—are in a unique position of power over

> "Over time, as rhetoricians highjack a word for their persuasive uses, loaded terms become inflammatory and polarizing and eventually lose their value in rational discussion of important topics. In this manner, the original intent and descriptive usefulness of the term becomes extinct."

---

[1] Kreger, C. David. "Homo sapiens." Archeology.info. 2008. (April 24, 2009) www.archaeologyinfo.com/homosapiens.htm

[2] Lovgren, Stefan. "Chimps, Humans 96 Percent the Same, Gene Study Finds." National Geographic News. Aug. 31, 2005. (April 24, 2009) http://news.nationalgeographic.com/news/2005/08/0831_050831_chimp_genes.html

those who are less skilled. That power is the power of *persuasion*.

Rhetoric is the use of language for persuasive effect and history abounds with examples of the pen being mightier than the sword. Often, key words will grow to define entire philosophies as one side or another of any given argument lay claim to terms. Examples include such words as *conservative, progressive, pro-choice, pro-life, disadvantaged,* etc. These words eventually become "loaded" and useful only in a combative sense. Loaded language attempts to influence the listener or reader by appealing to emotion, not reason.[3] Certain terms become so loaded that they literally become "code" for other concepts, such as the words *gay* and *straight*. Over time, as rhetoricians highjack a word for their persuasive uses, loaded terms become inflammatory and polarizing and eventually lose their value in rational discussion of important topics. In this manner, the original intent and descriptive usefulness of the term becomes *extinct*.

Professionalism is in danger of this fate. This is a problem because currently we have no other word to replace it.

In an attempt to sustain the usefulness of the term *professionalism*, or perhaps frame it for the first time for those who have never given it much thought, let's take a brief historical journey. Our purpose will be to seek and understand the roots of professional excellence as well as the reasons behind its decline in the modern era.

---

[3] Anthony Weston (2000). *A Rulebook for Arguments*. Hackett Publishing. p. 6.

A brief history of professionalism

The word *professional* itself comes to us, like most of our words, from the Latin, through Medieval French and into Olde and Middle English. We'll start with the root *profess*, which comes from the Latin word *profiteor*, "to acknowledge, confirm, promise, confess." The original term was used to refer to those who were seeking to become part of a religious order. According to the Oxford English Dictionary, considered the authoritative dictionary of the English language, the first recorded occurrence of "professional" was circa 1420, and it did indeed refer to "pertaining or making entrance into a religious order." Tracing the use of the term through the next few hundred years seems to indicate that the early meaning of a *profession* was some type of *solemn oath*, along the lines of what we might use the words "vow" or "promise" for in modern language. And it is this obligatory sense of the word that is carried into the first trade organizations.

The birth of the professions

The birth of the professions can be traced to initial specialization of craftsman that predates written language itself. It is clear from observation of stone tools and ancient architectures that groups of commonly skilled craftsmen existed long before the dawn of the written word. Stone carvers, lance makers, bow makers, and early architects all practiced common skills across great regions, and over time, these skills migrated to other tribes and locations.

One can speculate that these skills were transferred generationally from father and mother to son and daughter. However, when the workforce needed to be expanded to meet the survival demands of the tribe or clan, some form of specialized training was developed. It would not do to have a limited supply of arrowheads or crooked spears and arrows when the neighboring tribe showed up looking to expand their hunting grounds and take a few of your women and children.

> "It would not be long until skilled craftsmen became aware of their unique value and organized."

Early professionalism had more to do with competitive advantage than defense, as the tribes with the best weapons makers were far more likely to go on the offensive and expand <u>their</u> hunting grounds. Although the Hollywood version of historical conquests focuses on courageous warriors and insightful Chiefs, the capabilities of those warriors were largely defined by the types and numbers of the weapons they wielded.

There is a well-known axiom in military science that says that *amateurs talk tactics while professionals study logistics*. Then—as now—true power comes from the ability to equip, train, and sustain the military functions of the tribe, clan, or nation to protect and expand their territories and influence.

As a result of this logistical requirement, talented individuals with a desirable skill set were given special social status due to their unique value to the tribe or clan in which they functioned. Their time and efforts were uniquely valuable, and it is likely the arrowhead makers and horse trainers did not have to plow or plant the fields, haul water, or sew buffalo hides for tents. They spent their time doing what was important, manufacturing and <u>improving</u> the capabilities that made their society stronger. In this manner, a set of skills became a *trade*, and the fundamental concepts of supply and demand began to drive the evolution of early professionalism.

It would not be long until skilled craftsmen became aware of their unique value and organized. In pre-industrial cities, craftsmen began to form associations based on their trades. Over time, these crafts included masons, textile workers, carpenters, carvers, and glass workers. Typically, these early organizations resembled fraternities which controlled secrets; the arts and so-called "mysteries of their craft."[4] Often, the founders were free independent master craftsmen who recognized both the power of their specialized expertise as well as the vulnerability associated with allowing anyone and everyone to obtain it. At this point in history, the relationship between supply and demand becomes more complex and takes on another dimension.

Craftsmen in the early centuries A.D. through the Middle Ages understood that the best means for ensuring lifelong employment and earnings was to limit the supply of skilled tradesmen. However, to make their case for limiting who could ply their specialization without appearing to be simply money grubbing capitalists, they needed another leg to stand on. That leg was *quality*.

The rise of the guilds

The creation of the first true professional organizations (discounting religious orders) began to emerge over 2,000 years ago. There is considerable evidence of associations of skilled craftsmen in ancient China, the Middle East, and Europe as early as 200 B.C. The guilds

---

[4] Weyrauch, Thomas. *Craftsmen and their Associations in Asia, Africa and Europe.* Wettenberg/Germany, VVB Laufersweiler; 1999

served several purposes, but when searching for the primary reason for their formation, it is instructive that the term *guild* evolved from the Saxon word *gilden*, meaning "to pay."

However, there is little doubt that in an era where nearly all learning was based upon hands-on experience, the spin from the guilds toward society was less about compensation and more about preserving high levels of service and production. Guild officials pointed out that it was vitally important to match tradecraft masters and likely apprentices through monitored learning since, in many cases, the needed skills took many years to acquire.⁵ In this manner, the early guilds were among the first to establish formal standards for training of craftsmen and quality of product. A hierarchy and progression of craftsmen soon followed.

> "The guilds served several purposes, but when searching for the primary reason for their formation, it is instructive that the term guild evolved from the Saxon word gilden, meaning 'to pay.'"

> A hierarchy existed in large guilds. *Masters* were full members who usually owned their own workshops, retail outlets, or trading vessels. Masters employed *journeymen*, who were laborers who worked for wages on short term contracts or a daily basis (hence the term journeyman, from the French word for *day*). *Journeymen* hoped to one day advance to the level of master. To do this, journeymen usually had to save enough money to open a workshop and pay for admittance, or if they were lucky, receive a workshop through marriage or inheritance.

---

⁵ S. R. Epstein and Maarten Prak, eds. *Guilds, Innovation and the European Economy, 1400–1800.* Cambridge University Press, 2008

Masters also supervised *apprentices*, who were usually boys in their teens who worked for room, board, and perhaps a small stipend in exchange for a vocational education. Both guilds and government regulated apprenticeships, usually to ensure that masters fulfilled their part of the apprenticeship agreement. Terms of apprenticeships varied, usually lasting from five to nine years.[6]

Hence, early precursors to professionalism evolved around the dual commercial considerations of compensation through control of supply and demand, and quality control. Guilds were made up by experienced and confirmed experts, as well as novices. Before a novice could rise to the level of mastery, he had to go through a schooling period. To keep a tight lid on so-called "trade secrets," apprentices would typically not learn more than the most basic techniques until they were trusted by their peers to keep the guild's or company's secrets. Most importantly to our discussion of professionalism, the guilds created significant advances in the social capital of graduated training and standards, shared norms, common information, and known and approved sanctions for poor performance.

> "The guilds created significant advances in the social capital of graduated training and standards, shared norms, common information, and known and approved sanctions for poor performance."

In spite of its apparent merits, the guild system's dual roles of compensation control and quality assurance became unbalanced (I bet you can guess in what direction), and the entire system came under fire beginning in the renaissance era and continuing through

---

[6] Richardson, Gary. *Medieval Guilds*. Economic History Association. Found at http://eh.net/encyclopedia/article/richardson.guilds

their eventual demise in the industrial revolution. Although there are still many guild-like organizations, such as the state Bar Associations that govern the standards of conduct for the legal profession, those that remain are mere shadows of the power and influence once wielded by these powerful organizations.

The fall of the guilds

Over time, the focus on economic protection proved to be undoing of the guilds. Sheilagh Ogilvie, a Professor of Economic History at the University of Cambridge, argues that the guilds' focus progressively shifted away from quality and training and almost exclusively towards protective compensation and ideological control. This negatively affected quality, skills, and innovation, and the growing middle class recognized it. The guild system was targeted because they appeared to oppose free trade and hinder business development among those who would develop tradecraft into successful industries. Modern trade organizations would do well to heed this lesson of history.

Dr. Ogilvie maintains that the guilds persisted as long as they did only because they redistributed resources to politically powerful

> "With the fall of the guilds came the need for some type of regulator to fill the void in quality control and training requirements that were once provided by trade associations. This void was eventually filled by the creation of state-sponsored regulators."

merchants.[7] Calls for disbanding the guilds came from such diverse points of view as Jean-Jacques Rousseau, Adam Smith, and even Karl Marx. By the middle of the 19th century, the guild system had been replaced in favor of free trade policies and laws. This led to another challenge to the evolution of professionalism, one that persists to this day.

The rise of the regulator

With the fall of the guilds came the need for some type of regulator to fill the void in quality control and training requirements that were once provided by trade associations. This void was eventually filled by the creation of state-sponsored regulators.[8] In an attempt to consolidate over 100 years of public administration into some relevance and clarity, suffice to say that the highest risk industries of greatest import got the initial set of weights and measures. Because this book is written primarily at the problem of faltering professionalism in western society, we will limit our analysis to what has occurred in this regard within the United States. It is important

> "In the United States, regulations began to flow rapidly into the vacuum of worker safety and consumer protection, a trend that continues to this day."

---

[7] Sheilagh C Ogilvie, *"Rehabilitating the Guilds: A Reply,"* Economic History Review vol 61 (2008), 175–182

[8] IMHO, the rise of the state-sponsored regulator merely gave rise to a new type of corruption, but one with no overseer. Although this is not true in all cases, the unhealthy trending of government oversight influenced too strongly by corporate interests exists to this day.

to note that the same model of state-sponsored regulation grew around the globe, from the former Soviet Union to the rim of the old British Empire. From Bombay to Baltimore, when the guilds shut down, the state took the reins.

In the United States, regulations began to flow rapidly into the vacuum of worker safety and consumer protection, a trend that continues to this day. In some cases, this was done at the federal level with organizations that crossed industrial boundaries and set minimum standards for safety but did little to enhance the training or professionalism that occurred under the master-apprentice scrutiny of the guild system. The Occupational Safety and Health Administration (OSHA) is an example of this type of organization, which sets and evaluates safety standards but does little more to fill the quality and training voids once supplied by master craftsmen.

In other cases, industry-specific organizations grew, such as the Federal Aviation Administration (FAA) and Mine Safety and Health Administration (MSHA). The case of the FAA is an interesting one in that at one point in its development, it had the dual (and competing) roles of promoting development of the aviation industry and also ensuring the safety of operations. At least the FAA was honest enough to acknowledge this conundrum openly, although following an embarrassing string of accidents the "dual role" of the FAA was *officially* abolished a few decades ago.

One example of how bad this government-industry oversight arrangement can get occurred between 2002 and 2006 within the U.S. Department of Interior Minerals Management Service (MMS), which oversees the compliance of oil and minerals contracts for the American taxpayer. According the Department of Interior Inspector General, government workers routinely engaged in sex and drug abuse with oil company employees and accepted thousands of dollars in gifts while handling billions of dollars' worth of energy contracts. The IG report went on to say that these employees, including the former head of the Denver division, repeatedly and "without remorse" violated ethics rules over a four-year period.

The official testimony of Acting Inspector General Mary Kendall told the House Committee on Natural Resources that

> ... her agency documented "programmatic weaknesses and egregious misconduct" at the Minerals and Management Services ... "While I neither condone nor excuse the behavior chronicled in this, our most recent report on MMS—gift-acceptance, fraternizing with industry, pornography, and other inappropriate materials on government computers, and lax handling of inspection forms—I am more concerned "about the environment in which these inspectors operate and the ease with which they move between industry and government."

Though the rise of the regulator was intended to fill the gaps to ensure consumer protection and worker safety, even those tasks of minimalist professionalism soon began to erode. Far too often, we see convincing evidence that the regulator falls into bed with the industry they are established to regulate.

This occurs for two reasons. First, most government regulators are groomed and hired upon "retirement" by the industry they were once overseeing. This sets up an unwholesome relationship where the regulator and industry dance in the final years of a government servant's career. A regulator who is seen as too harsh on a particular industry is unlikely to find lucrative employment upon his retirement,

> "Far too often, we see convincing evidence that the regulator falls into bed with the industry they are established to regulate."

whereas one who is more lenient in both policy creation and oversight is seen as just the type of liaison a private sector industry wants with the next generation of regulator.

Stalemate

Using the case of the FAA as an example, the economics of capitalism creates a stalemate of sorts where aviation operators aggressively fight nearly all attempts at additional regulation, while holding to the position that the status quo with regard to training and safety is satisfactory. While the regulator attempts to raise the bar, industry points to the fact that government mandates cost money and reduce profit. Furthermore, training to higher standards is seen by some as a competitive <u>disadvantage</u> if they are able to achieve required compliance at lower costs.

In summary, the rise of the regulator began the slow fall of professionalism as industries began to focus on minimum regulatory standards rather than mastery of their trade. In this environment, innovation in areas that would foster greater levels of professionalism ground to a halt. In some areas, other stakeholders arose in an attempt to fill the gap.

Breakthrough: The International Organization for Standardization (ISO)

At the risk of straying too far from the core topic of professionalism, it is worth noting that the last half century has given rise to significant accomplishment of mutually agreeable common standards in many areas.

Shortly following the Second World War, delegates from 25 countries met in London and decided to create a new international organization, of which the object would be "to facilitate the international coordination and unification of industrial standards."[9] The new organization, the International Organization for Standardization (ISO), began operations in February 1947. Since the development was led by the Swiss, the headquarters was placed in Geneva, Switzerland.

Since that time, more than 160 countries have joined forces to develop and publish over 18,000 voluntary international standards in technical fields. To date, no standards for *professionalism* are among them.

It may be time to remedy this oversight.

The official ISO website points to one critical missing piece of the professionalism challenge, the desire to bridge the gap between industry and government for the betterment of society at large.

> ISO is a nongovernmental organization that forms a bridge between the public and private sectors. On the one hand, many of its member institutes are part of the governmental structure

---

[9] *Friendship Among Equals: Recollections from the first fifty years of ISO.* www.iso.org

of their countries or are mandated by their government. On the other hand, other members have their roots uniquely in the private sector, having been set up by national partnerships of industry associations. Therefore, ISO enables a consensus to be reached on solutions that meet both the requirements of business and the broader needs of society. Standards make an enormous and positive contribution to most aspects of our lives. Standards ensure desirable characteristics of products and services such as quality, environmental friendliness, safety, reliability, efficiency, and interchangeability—and at an economical cost.[10]

While ISO has a definite bias towards technical standards associated with manufacturing, the idea of internationally codified and shared standards provides one model that may be worth serious consideration with nontechnical skills such as professionalism. We will discuss this in much greater detail in a later chapter.

In modern times, other stakeholders have also attempted to take up the slack left by the minimalist approach of the state regulator.

The vital role of organized labor

Industry-specific labor organizations also provide clues to the successful resurrection of professional standards of conduct. In several industries, trade organizations have stepped into the discussion, citing the need to have fully trained and certified workers to ensure consumer protection and safety.

---

[10] http://www.iso.org

The Air Line Pilots Association (ALPA) is one such organization that represents over 50,000 airline pilots. ALPA lists three primary objectives as its reason for being: *Airline safety and security, representation,* and *advocacy*.[11] In spite of the order that these objectives are listed, ALPA's driving objective is certainly the wellbeing and continued employment of its members, as indicated in its vision statement.

> The Air Line Pilots Association, International, will spare no effort to aggressively fight for the rights and needs of airline pilots. We will work together—across all segments and corporate brands—to restore our proud profession. We are committed to the principle that our profession is best served by unifying all pilots within our union and organizing all pilots within our profession. ALPA pilots must embody the values of solidarity, integrity, and tenacity as we work to accomplish the goals of the union. Leaders commit to identifying and aggressively addressing the concerns, aspirations, and ideas of our members and leaders will act decisively to move the pilots' agenda forward.[12]

Organized labor represents a real force in most industries, and ALPA clearly recognizes it is in the best interest of its members to promote safety, security, and a professional workforce. Towards that end, they have created an *Airline Pilot's Code of Ethics* that has multiple elements aimed at the core of professional conduct, a few examples of which are listed below.[13]

- An Air Line Pilot will keep uppermost in his mind that the safety,

---

[11] http://www.alpa.org
[12] ALPA's Vision, Strategic Goals & Initiatives. www.Alpa.org
[13] This is an abbreviated list used to highlight the elements of the code that point to core topic of *professionalism*.

comfort, and well-being of the passengers who entrust their lives to him are his first and greatest responsibility.

- He will never permit external pressures or personal desires to influence his judgment, nor will he knowingly do anything that could jeopardize flight safety.
- An Air Line Pilot will faithfully discharge the duty he owes the airline that employs him and whose salary makes possible his way of life. He will respect the officers, directors, and supervisors of his airline, remembering that respect does not entail subservience.
- He will faithfully obey all lawful directives given by his supervisors, but will insist and, if necessary, refuse to obey any directives that, in his considered judgment, are not lawful or will adversely affect flight safety.
- He will not knowingly falsify any log or record, nor will he condone such action by other crew members.
- He will remember that a full month's salary demands a full and fair month's work.
- He will give his airline, its officers, directors, and supervisors the full loyalty that is their due and will refrain from speaking ill of them.
- He will realize that he represents the airline to all who meet him and will at all times keep his personal appearance and conduct above reproach.
- An Air Line Pilot will remember that his is a profession heavily dependent on training during regular operations ... He will endeavor to instill in his crew a sense of pride and responsibility.
- He will not falsely or maliciously injure the professional

> "The Airline Pilot's Code of Ethics is powerful stuff, and ALPA is not alone among organized labor in its concern and promotion of professional standards."

reputation, prospects, or job security of another pilot, yet if he knows of professional incompetence or conduct detrimental to the profession or to ALPA, he will not shrink from revealing this to the proper authorities ...

- He will cooperate in the upholding of the profession by exchanging information and experience with his fellow pilots and by actively contributing to the work of professional groups and the technical press.

- To an Air Line Pilot, the honor of his profession is dear, and he will remember that his own character and conduct reflect honor or dishonor upon the profession.

- He will be a good citizen of his country, state, and community, taking an active part in their affairs, especially those dealing with the improvement of aviation facilities and the enhancement of air safety.

- He will conduct all his affairs in a manner that reflects credit on his profession.

The *Airline Pilot's Code of Ethics* is powerful stuff, and ALPA is not alone among organized labor in its concern and promotion of professional standards. However, even with carefully codified standards such as those created and advocated by ALPA, the problem for organized labor comes on the enforcement end of the spectrum. In most, if not all of organized labor, their leaders are elected and serve at the pleasure of the members. Few can gain or hold their respective leadership positions if their focus is on enforcement of professional standards. This limits their influence to one of advocacy.

If you are looking for an organization that not only clearly states and advocates elements of professionalism, but is also duty bound and legally empowered to enforce their professional standards, you have to belly up to the bar.

No more lawyer jokes

Most are aware that a *bar association* is a professional body of lawyers, usually organized at the state level. Some bar associations are responsible for the regulation of the legal profession in their jurisdiction; others are professional organizations dedicated to serving their members; in many cases, they are both. The American Bar Association's *Model Rules of Professional Conduct*[14] outline in a very specific manner what professional standards a practicing lawyer must maintain. More importantly, most states also articulate what happens if you do not.

The *Model Rules of Professional Conduct* covers a wide variety of topics from diligence to conflict of interest. Lawyers who do not meet these standards face disbarment at the hands of their own. But you have to behave in a pretty egregious manner to have disbarment sanctions invoked against you. In many ways, the bar associations are like the state sponsored regulators in that they establish minimum standards and enforce them reluctantly.

---

[14] http://www.americanbar.org/groups/professional_responsibility/publications/model_rules_of_professional_conduct/model_rules_of_professional_conduct_table_of_contents.html

The present

So what have we learned from this short time travel experience?

First, we discovered that the roots of professionalism run back over a thousand years, winding their way from religious orders who took vows, through trade guilds who structured and enforced standards set by Master Craftsmen, and more recently into state-sponsored regulators and organized labor.

Secondly, we see that in each of these cases, *professionalism* became a bit of a sideshow, never receiving the same prime time billing as the principle goals or objectives of these organizations, which were usually financial or protectionist in nature. Or, more recently that *professionalism* is only defined by minimum standards, which are often stated in various forms but seldom seriously advocated as a standard and even more rarely enforced.

We discovered the rise of a global standardization organization in the middle of the 20th century (ISO), but unfortunately, it currently only deals with *technical* standards and measures.

Finally, we see the effect of the information age, where breaches of professional conduct reach millions in moments, resulting in the erosion of trust in some of our key industries such as health care, public transportation, finance, and education.

So, where do we go from here?

The future

There is little doubt that we are on the precipice of major changes in the way we deal with both the ideal and the active practice of *professionalism*. Reality shows and the media (old and new) clamor for the next salacious story of a trusted professional gone bad, whetting the appetite of the public, who in turn demand that politicians and regulators to "do something about it."

Public trust is a fickle thing. It is manipulated by marketers, politicians, and others, and there is little doubt that in the absence of a proactive effort to deal with the perceptions and reality of unprofessional behaviors, regulation will flow into the perceived vacuum.

> "There is little doubt that we are on the precipice of major changes in the way we deal with both the ideal and the active practice of professionalism."

The choice we face as professionals in all industries is whether we are going to drive this bus or ride in it. In our next chapter, we begin to rough in the structure of the "new professionalism," in a bold attempt to take control and design our future with regards to professionalism in 21st century business and government.

"Don't live down to expectations."

Wendy Wasserstein, Playwright

Chapter 3

Aren't We <u>All</u> Professionals?

"Obviously, your definition and mine are somewhat different."
Robert Sumwalt, National Transportation Safety Board Member

AREN'T WE ALL PROFESSIONALS?

The cult of self-esteem is getting people killed.

The quote by National Transportation Safety Board Member Robert Sumwalt on the previous page comes from a story he tells of trying to provide constructive feedback to an airline Captain following a less than perfect flight a few years back. The Captain did not welcome the unsolicited feedback and responded defensively by stating that "we are all professionals here." Robert's response about their respective definitions of professionalism being "somewhat different" cuts to the heart of the issue.

Far too many fragile egos have been constructed over the past few decades by a cultural drift that has valued self-esteem above true competence. In a society where every little leaguer

> "When these fragile, homogeneous, *mediocritters* (critters of mediocrity) meet the uncertainty and unforgiving nature of the real world, they underperform, and in the aftermath, blame others or the situation."

gets a trophy and grade inflation has made over half of the kids in some Middle Schools honor roll students, true excellence has been devalued to the point where few recognize it and fewer still think it is even important. In fact, many see those who do excel above the cultural norms as damaging to the peer group or even society as a whole. In Australia, they have a name for this phenomenon. It is called the "tall poppy syndrome."[1]

When these fragile, homogeneous, *mediocritters* (critters of mediocrity) meet the uncertainty and unforgiving nature of the real world, they underperform, and in the aftermath, blame others or the situation. Having never been taught to accept responsibility, they resort to excuse making in order to preserve their precious self-esteem.

This situation results in a state of affairs where individuals in positions of immense responsibility (surgeons, pilots, law enforcement, financial executives, etc.) are left to "roll their own" when it comes to evaluating themselves against vague or nonexistent standards of professionalism, sometimes with tragic and irreversible results. In the aftermath of these often fatal events, the white flag of "the inevitability of human error" is typically hoisted. People die in so called "accidents" but the living, who may have caused it—or could have prevented it—get to preserve their self-esteem, because after all, "to err is human."[2]

It need not be so. Or at least not so often.

---

[1] The tallest poppy is the first to be cut down at harvest time.
[2] For a full discussion of the fallacy of the "to err is human" white flag, read *Blue Threat: Why to Err is Inhuman*. Kern, Pygmy Books, 2009.

"Mediocrity is the new excellence"

The ability to differentiate between levels of performance is one of the most telling attributes of an expert in any field. Some high performers intuitively develop this skill, but in the absence of agreed upon standards, most are left to guess or debate *excellence* as a matter of opinion. Some will even find a bit of humor in the rhetoric, as in the case that follows.

America's military academies are one of the few places in our world where excellence should still mean something. The nation's best and brightest compete to get in these prestigious leadership laboratories and then spend four years in extremely rigorous military, leadership, and academic preparation. They also know full well that they are heading into a hostile world filled with those who will test their wits and readiness with bullets aimed with hostile intent.

The US Air Force Academy in Colorado Springs is one of these institutions.[3] Last year, while attending an event at the Academy, I saw an upper class cadet with a yellow and black button on his backpack that read *Mediocrity is the new excellence*. I had to ask.

In our short discussion, the young man explained to me that the Academy (and Air Force as a whole) has three *core values*:

Integrity first

Service before self

Excellence in all we do

He stated that he had been somewhat disappointed with several of his recent training experiences and the yellow button was just

---

[3] Dr. Kern served as an Associate Professor and Director of Military History at the USAF Academy from 1995 to 2000. His two sons also attended USAFA.

> "Elitism has a place in our world. There is nothing wrong with people who seek to be better than the rest, to stand above the crowd."

his way of quietly and humorously protesting the decline in excellence he was witnessing.[4] His point was that if he followed the first core value (integrity), he was duty bound to tell the truth about the failures of the third (excellence).

Clever kid—he gets it. But not all see the value of performing to the highest possible standards, of becoming truly elite.

In praise of elitism

Elitism has a place in our world. There is nothing wrong with people who seek to be better than the rest, to stand above the crowd. I'm not talking about the egocentric jerks that have too much pride and narcissistic, self-inflated egos, but rather the quietly confident expert who has earned the right to be considered in the top 1% of their respective field. If we hope to reverse the decline of professionalism we are witnessing in our society, we need more, not less, of this type of elitism to lead the way.

The fact that most fields haven't (yet) defined the standards to identify this group does not alter the fact that these high performing

---

[4] This is not a commentary on the overall excellence of the Air Force Academy, which provides one of the finest undergraduate educations in the world while truly producing world class leaders of character. On the contrary, the fact that this young man thought the lack of excellence in some areas worthy of comment, attests to the type of leader being built there.

experts exist. They are not always the ones that are known to the world, or that hold prestigious positions of authority, *but they are known to their peers.*

"Standards measure with discrimination, standards rank from top to bottom, standards expose posers."

Hard opposition from the "comfortably mediocre"

While the elite have intuitively figured out what it is that makes a true expert and have voluntarily followed the path, the comfortably mediocre despise refined standards of performance. It doesn't allow the wiggle room for claiming greatness through volume, position, or imitation.

Standards measure with discrimination, standards rank from top to bottom, standards expose posers. In a world without standards of professionalism, everyone is free to stake their claim. Everyone gets a trophy. All the kids are on the honor roll. I'm OK, you're OK—and the death toll rises.

So the tough question becomes *how can we begin to turn the ship of mediocrity towards higher levels of professionalism in a culture where it has been devalued in so many places for so long?* Perhaps there is a way to allow nearly all to claim the title *professional* while simultaneously raising the bar.

Roughing in the structure

As we begin to define and refine the temple of professionalism, we will work from general to specific. In previous chapters, we have outlined the challenge we face and traced the rise and fall of this vital cornerstone of excellence. Now we turn to the challenge of creating the future.

Let's begin with an obvious fact of change management. It will be nearly impossible to convince those who are currently clinging to their self-esteem by virtue of their employment in a particular field to abandon the self-appointed title of *professional*. This is true no matter what level of excellence or compliance they are currently performing at. So to deal with this challenge, greater definition and discrimination is required under the *professionalism* umbrella.

For this purpose, we are creating three stepping stones to world class performance, which I will cleverly label *Professionalism Levels I, II, and III. Level I is mere membership in a career field*—a definition many seem to be holding to.

Level I professionalism – Membership

To earn a living in a given profession, you have to meet certain selection criteria and then find someone willing to give you a job. This type of preparation usually involves some academic and vocational training and represents the first cut. Successful candidates have been competitively vetted to standards that unsuccessful candidates for the job did not meet. At this point, you have reached Level I—admittance to a career field—and may claim the title of *Level I professional* under the following definition:

> **pro•fes•sion•al•ism.** *Noun.* A professional is a member of a vocation founded upon specialized education and training.

AREN'T WE ALL PROFESSIONALS?   69

At this point, we have legitimized entry level professionalism of those who claim,

"I'm a pro because I earn a paycheck in this industry."

Clearly, Level I leaves much to be desired, as it doesn't even require continued maintenance to the same standards that were required for selection. In today's litigious society, hiring is easy, firing hard. As a result, there are many that see the day they get hired into their dream job as the day they can kick back and relax. The days of having to prove themselves are over and a natural decline sets in. It has been said that a job offer in a great company is the place where high achievement often goes to die—or at least to sleep. People relax, and so long as there are no unwanted outcomes, standards are also relaxed. Noncompliant easy street.

The performance of Level I professionals in this state of professional suspended animation often declines over time, as the day-to-day experience of "no harm – no foul" routines leads to the normalization of deviance and routine noncompliance. We see or hear about examples of low level professionals behaving unprofessionally in this manner nearly every day. Clearly, something more is needed to address this natural decline.

"In today's fast paced, do more with less business world, routine noncompliance is often ignored by task saturated supervisory personnel and the system at large."

Our second definition raises the bar from *mere membership to Level II Professionalism – full compliance.*

Level II professionalism – Full compliance

Contrary to popular belief, noncompliance is rampant in modern industry and government,[5] as highly experienced personnel frequently "bend the rules" for a wide variety of reasons without remorse or serious consequence. Most noncompliance is of a "lesser crime" nature and does not often rise to the level of newsworthiness or action inside organizations. In today's fast paced, do more with less business world, routine noncompliance is often ignored by task saturated supervisory personnel and the system at large. Yet there is little doubt that if not corrected, noncompliance will progressively erode the integrity and quality of an organization and its product or service. It is also the first step in a normalization of deviance sequence that can result in far greater deviations with significantly more severe results and consequences.

With this realization, we arrive at *Level II Professionalism*, where men and women of integrity refuse to look the other way and hold themselves and others to a higher standard.

> **pro•fes•sion•al•ism.** *Noun.* Professionalism is the adherence to a set of values comprising statutory professional obligations and formally agreed codes of conduct.

Level II professionals stake their claim in this manner:

> *"I'm a pro because I meet and maintain the standards."*

Although Level II pros are a cut above their complacent counterparts resting at Level I, the idea that *routine compliance* covers the full scope of professionalism seems to be lacking something; sort of a

---

[5] For a full discussion of the noncompliance challenge, see "The Myth of Compliance," Chapter 5 in *Blue Threat: Why to Err is Inhuman*. Kern, Pygmy Books, 2009.

lite beer version of the full bodied thing itself. Make no mistake; if most organizations could get all their workers to *Level II*, they would be making a great stride forward.

But keep in mind that the standards we currently live with were primarily established following the fall of the guilds and the rise of the regulator, which means they are *minimum* standards for safety and consumer protection. What about the pursuit of quality? What about excellence?

The final stepping stone of elevated professional performance raises the bar to *Level III – empowered accountability*, where the individual continuously seeks to go above and beyond established standards in the pursuit of excellence in all areas.

> "Level III defines the essence of a *professionalist*—a relatively new term that defines the passion and practice of individuals who seek the highest standards above and beyond what the regulations require or that are expected of them."

Level III professionalism – Full empowerment and accountability

Level III professionalism is both a career spanning growth experience as well as a nearby and near term destination for all who wish to raise the bar on their performance. A Level III pro is an elite performer who strives daily to meet the following definition of professionalism:

pro•fes•sion•al•ism. *Noun.* Meticulous adherence to undeviating courtesy, honesty, and responsibility in one's dealings with customers and associates, plus a level of excellence that goes over and above the commercial considerations and legal requirements.

Note that there is nothing in this definition that requires 20 years of experience. Level III is achievable by novices and highly experienced workers alike—albeit at different levels of technical expertise. These elite performers make their claim as professionals in this manner.

> *"I'm a pro because I am doing all I can to be the best I can and further the objectives of my peers, my organization, and the industry as a whole."*

Level III defines the essence of a ***professionalist***—a relatively new term that defines the passion and practice of individuals who seek the highest standards above and beyond what the regulations require or that are expected of them. These individuals are not only interested in being the best that they can be in their profession; they are interested in improving the profession itself.

Professionalism Levels I through III are illustrated in the following figure.

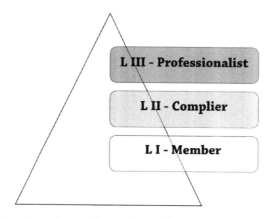

Professionalism Levels I, II, and III

With these definitions running in our mental background, let's see if we can pull the mask off a few wanna-bes.

Unmasking pseudo professionals

We all know a few of these people; strutters and posers who for some reason or another have convinced a few in the system that they are high achievers. The purpose of this section is emphatically NOT to label individuals, but rather to make you aware that a holistic set of professional standards will unmask these pretenders and hopefully lead them to more fully develop into consummate pros. If any of these descriptions make you a bit uneasy, so much the better. Self-identification and self-correction are always the best paths to improvement.

The empty suit

All image, with little beneath the surface—these are the guys and gals that look great doing nothing. The empty suit loves to participate on committees and attend functions. They crave "face time" with the boss. Later in the book, we will undress the empty suit using the full set of assessment tools we will develop over the next few chapters.

There are a few positive things we can learn from the empty suit, including how to master many of the nontechnical skills such as communication, persuasion, and professional image that many hard working professionals lack.

Professional by proximity

There are actually two versions of this pseudo professional. The first is the individual who claims high professional status because of the company or organization they work for. For example, recently I ran into a colleague who was more than willing to give me financial advice on my company (even though I had not asked). "If you're looking for advice on where you should be putting your resources, I work for a Fortune 100 corporation so let me give you a few tips." This gentleman with the altruistic intent was actually a software installer, but that did not seem to bother him in the least as he explained in great detail what his company would do in our shoes. Just because you work for Berkshire-Hathaway does not mean you possess the financial wisdom of owner Warren Buffet.

The second version of professional by proximity is where in the organization you work. It might be the world headquarters or the executive offices on the 50th floor, but this pseudo pro hints at knowing inside secrets that the ordinary employee does not have access to. Keep in mind that lots of people work at the world headquarters or on the 50th floor. Very few ever see the inside of the boardroom, and some are just making copies or making sure the coffee pots stay full.

Professional by pedigree

Closely related to the *professional by proximity* is the *professional by pedigree*. These are the individuals who came from somewhere else, either a prestigious university or previous posting, and claim superiority from past associations. This is one step up from the proximity claim in that it usually means that some point in their careers they completed a tough degree program or were a part of a highly successful project or program. However, keep in mind that although someone has a Yale law degree or a certificate from the *Kennedy School* at Harvard, it may have little bearing on their current position or the task at hand.

Professionals by pedigree seldom fail to mention their association when making any new acquaintance and provide frequent visual (certificates and diplomas on the wall) and verbal reminders.

Don't misunderstand; there is nothing wrong with being a proud alumnus. I am tremendously honored to have degrees from Albion College, Northern Michigan University, the US Army Command and General Staff College, and Texas Tech. The problem arises when these past associations are used to provide "evidence" of current professional capabilities. In the words of the famous baseball pitcher Satchel Paige, "It ain't about what you used to was."

One hit wonder

The one hit wonder is the professional equivalent of the 80's rock band Tommy Tutone.[6] These individuals were fortunate enough to have had a major professional success in their past, but little since. One hit wonders come in different levels of professional validity. For example, if their one hit was discovering wormholes after 20 years

---

[6] *Tommy Tutone* is best known for its 1982 hit "867-5309/Jenny", which peaked at #4 on the Billboard Hot 100. The song became so popular that people in the United States to this day dial this telephone number and ask for Jenny. It is also a classic example of a "brain itch" song that is nearly impossible to get out of your head once you've heard it. For those of you who need help, try "Get that damn song out of my head" at unhearit.com.

of exhausting research, that is pretty legit. But if their claim to professional fame is something of a shorter duration or as a part of a team, such as "I was part of the project team that rewrote all the company job descriptions in the mid 90's," that's a bit weak.

The point to all of these descriptions of pseudo professionals is that they are all probably well-meaning workers in search of a professional identity. In the absence of standards, who can argue?

> "In spite of the seriousness of the professionalism challenges we face, we have reason to be optimistic."

Reasons to be optimistic

In spite of the seriousness of the professionalism challenges we face, we have reason to be optimistic. We have faced serious nontechnical challenges before in our society. Examples include:

- In the 1960's, 70's, and 80's, Edward Deming saw that improved quality in manufacturing systems could be a huge competitive advantage in the coming global marketplace. He was ignored in the US and took his message on how to achieve world class quality to Japan. It took 20 years for it to come back home, but by then many US companies were already hopelessly behind and are still struggling to catch up.

- In the 1970's and early 80's, it was determined that issues of aircrew coordination, communication, and authority gradient were behind a series of highly publicized airline accidents. In response, the industry created CRM (cockpit/crew resource management) to address the challenge. At the time, these programs were considered way out of the box and resisted by many. But three decades later, they have proven to be highly effective and are now mainstream parts of every professional pilot's training.

- In the 1990's, MIT professor Peter Senge introduced us to *The Fifth Discipline* – systems thinking which led to a revolution of integration.

- Some suggest that due to the past success of these quality, team training, and systemic solutions that they are also where we should turn for answers to the *professionalism* challenge. I respectfully disagree. While it is possible to use a standard flat blade screwdriver to remove a Phillips screw, it is generally not a good idea. You need to use the right tool for the job. Each of the previous "out of the box" solutions relied on interpersonal and systemic change. The current challenge of noncompliance and unprofessionalism must be addressed *intrapersonally*—a discussion we must have within ourselves. But like the previous successes, these empowered accountability skills are not intuitive—they must be learned, practiced, and applied.

It is time for another out of the box solution.

Summary

Six months before he would be struck down by an assassin's bullet, President John F. Kennedy told the 1962 graduating class at Yale, "We must move on from reassuring repetition of stale phrases to a new, difficult, but essential confrontation with reality." Those of us in modern industry and government officials would do well to heed this advice. We have to challenge the assumption that "we are all professionals" on three levels.

First, as a society, we must recall that hard work and sacrifice is what made us the envy of the world. Turning the big ship of professionalism around will take considerable effort. Perhaps, in the quest for the technological high ground, Western society may have lost track of one of its professional touchstones—uncompromising attention to detail and the rigorous pursuit of excellence.

Second, as industries, we must get out from behind defensive positions and admit (at least to ourselves) that we have a professionalism problem. This is especially difficult for the public relations and legal professionals inside our decision teams to accept of get behind. This resistance must be overcome.

Finally, we must engage as individuals. The really good news is that because of the difficulties and reluctance cited at the societal and industry levels, the individual is uniquely empowered to leapfrog over peers who stick with the status quo. By learning and applying the profound knowledge of the Level III professional outlined in the chapters that follow, you can personally choose to become ten feet tall in a six foot world.

In our next chapter, we begin the heavy lifting of defining the new standards.

"You have been weighed. You have been measured; . . . and you have been found wanting."

Count Ulrich von Liechtenstein

(played by Heath Ledger in "A Knight's Tale")

Chapter 4

Setting the Bar: The New Professionalism

"In God we trust; all others bring data."

Edward Deming

SETTING THE BAR: THE NEW PROFESSIONALISM

If you are playing to win, the game has to have rules and someone needs to keep score.

So far, we have seen why many stakeholders in the professionalism discussion do not want to keep score, or don't think they need to. Hopefully by now we have seen what their motivations are, or in the case of complacent Level I professionals, what their motivations *aren't*. In either case, their positions on the topic are not showstoppers for those who truly desire to excel as a Level III professional.

This chapter lays out the rules of the game: the system of professionalism, definitions of key elements, behavioral standards, and weights and measures. It is followed by a chapter on the methods of *deliberate practice* and then six chapters that drill deep into each sub-domain of professionalism with the tools for adding some serious professionalism horsepower.

But before we start keeping score, let's make sure we are tuned into a couple serious risks to this entire effort.

The yin and yang of keeping score (hazards of assessment)

As we learned from the ISO and quality revolutions, standards are critical and weights and measures must be developed, agreed upon, and shared if we hope to drive and sustain long term improvement. However, unlike ISO standards or *Malcolm Baldrige* quality criteria,[1] this effort is not about measuring the tensile strength of a widget or the quality processes of an assembly line—we are talking about the values, attitudes, and behaviors of *real people on the job*, and therefore, must seriously consider all of the potential benefits and consequences of performance rating in advance.

If the professionalism revolution is to survive infancy, we must be diligent from the very beginning in establishing the answers to three game-breaking questions:

1. How will we measure professionalism?
2. Who does the measuring and receives the data?
3. How will professionalism data be used?

If we get these wrong, we put the entire professionalism initiative at risk. Let me state this in even more forceful and clear terms.

If we mismanage how the data generated by the new assessments are used, we will lose the opportunity to leverage the current momentum towards enhanced professionalism for a generation or more, perhaps forever.

---

[1] The *Malcolm Baldrige National Quality Award* recognizes U.S. organizations in the business, health care, education, and nonprofit sectors for performance excellence. The *Baldrige Award* is the only formal recognition of the performance excellence of both public and private U.S. organizations given by the President of the United States.

At the heart of this concern are two concepts inherent in all change management efforts; *willpower* and *trust*. If you have picked up this book and gotten this far, the spark of self-improvement is at least glowing, if not yet burning brightly. The will to improve is present, but there is one other major potential roadblock.

Trust is in short supply in many industries and organizations. So let's address this concern first and answer the three game breakers in reverse order.

How should professionalism data be used?

Skeptics, cynics, and barristers will immediately notice that there was a subtle change to this question from the numbered list that preceded it, as the word *will* was replaced with *should*. Make no mistake, the power to measure human performance associated with a lightning rod concept like *professionalism* can work for good or ill intent. Since neither the reader nor I will be sitting on the Board of Directors for every organization that chooses to use this new approach, strong recommendations and cautionary statements regarding the use of professionalism rating tools are warranted.

The first obvious point is that there are no concerns at all about tools used for personal growth and <u>self</u>-assessment. These instruments, including the assessments and personal inventory tools contained in this book, are your private data, unless you choose to share them.

However, we have developed many assessment tools to help organizations understand and shape their professionalism cultures, and it is here where the data has the potential to be misused.

The following recommendations are made for any who plan to use the Going Pro assessments in an organizational setting.

- *Professionalism data should be viewed as a tool for selection, advancement, or improvement, not as a tool for disciplinary actions.* There are multiple professionalism assessment instruments currently available for organizational use and mentorship programs, as well as a set of behavioral markers for real-time observation and feedback by trained observers whose sole purpose is coaching for improvement. All of these tools require a short training period to ensure they are not misunderstood or misused.

- *Professionalism data should be de-identified at the level of the individual before being placed into an aggregate.* Aggregated data can be a powerful tool to feed culture change efforts. When group data is combined to illustrate the professionalism strengths and weaknesses, targeted efforts for improvement are possible. For example, professionalism data from one part of an organization that is achieving better results might be used to establish key areas that should be codified and shared as a professionalism best practice (PBP).

  Conversely, underperforming subcultures can be analyzed through the lens of professional conduct in a troubleshooting mode. Some have even suggested that an intra-industry approach might be possible that establishes professionalism benchmarks between companies, in the same manner that *J.D. Powers and Associates* currently addresses quality and customer satisfaction.

All of these approaches are reasonable if—<u>and only if—the data is de-identified at the level of each individual to protect the privacy and rights of those who are participating in the improvement effort</u>.

- *Ideally, professionalism data should be used for professional development or continuous improvement, not as a risk mitigation or loss prevention tool.* This is a tricky one that relates to our discussion in Chapter 1 about who has historically discovered acts of unprofessionalism. Typically, when professionalism hits our radar, it's a result of some egregious act that is a safety, profitability, or public perception concern. Therefore, the ball for fixing the problem is most often thrown to risk mitigation or loss prevention staff. While appropriate in a reactive sense, this results in a "don't be unprofessional" fix rather than a proactive drive for higher performance.

  In most organizations, the ball should be handed to whoever is responsible for selection and professional development, which are typically human resource or continuous improvement taskings. As a continuous improvement tool, these data should be integrated and analyzed along with other quality data (six sigma, lean, continuing excellence programs, etc.) in a holistic analytical package.

  With all due respect to my operations colleagues (especially in aviation), we tend to look at data from a troubleshooting perspective, and get into a "let's fix this quick and move on" mode. Others take a longer view, and the likelihood of permanent change is enhanced.

Limits of data use must be clearly spelled out to build the first layer of trust. But process and procedures are only as good as those who implement them, which leads to our next questions.

Who does the measuring? Who sees the data?

Data is just data, coldly neutral until such time as someone adds meaning through interpretation. For this reason, the selection and training of personnel who will interpret and see this data is of paramount importance. This is true *even if the only one who sees it is you* as part of a self-improvement effort.

As you will soon see, the means to observe, collect, and quantify professionalism data with great discrimination is now at hand. But as we discussed earlier, many will strongly resist any assessment effort that might provide important but negative feedback. This is because they are still operating under the influence of political correctness bred from the cult of self-esteem. Because of a phenomenon known as *confirmation bias*, most will initially look for subjective evidence that supports our preconceptions—that everything is fine with our own state of professionalism. Quantitative assessments do a better job of taking confirmation bias out of the equation.

Early adopters of the new professionalism must be mindful of this resistance and reach out with assurances that the data will be handled by those with proper training, an improvement mindset, and clearly established and agreed upon limits.

What we learned from Deming

I realize that citing the great Edward Deming is <u>so</u> last century, but the example that he set over five decades to drive the global *quality improvement* revolution is worth a brief moment of study.

As Deming set out to empower the change management piece of the quality revolution, he led by training and convincing managers and leaders who had the most to gain, but ironically would be his greatest resistors. Deming advocated that all managers, leaders, and change agents needed to have what he called a *system of profound knowledge*, consisting of four parts:[2]

- *Appreciation of a system:* Understanding the overall processes involved with the new way of doing things was step one. Once the system is understood, trust in the data and improvement it provides begins to build. This will be just as critical with the professionalism revolution. We will need to understand the system and its benefits to gain acceptance of the concepts and belief in the potential of positive change.

- *Knowledge of variation:* This is the discriminatory aspect made available through use of new tools, which allows for deeper understanding with more finely tuned and targeted data. The tools for measuring our professionalism status will make critical distinctions between Level I, II, and III professionals, and empower personal and organizational change.

- *Theory of knowledge:* There is a strong anti-intellectual streak in modern business, but we must comprehend the terms and concepts that will be made available, as well as the limits of what can be discovered and known through their use. High achievers

---
[2] Deming, W. Edwards (1986). *Out of the Crisis*. MIT Press.

are quick studies, and they often want to "skip the theory" and get right to the tools. When it comes to change of this magnitude, we will only be as committed as we are convinced of the validity and reliability of the information being provided. The new professionalism requires new knowledge. We must not fight it.

- *Knowledge of psychology:* These are the concepts of human nature, such as readiness, learning theory, and change resistance that come into play as new information is applied to improve performance. Awareness of these barriers to change was critical to the quality movement and will be just as critical to the professionalism movement.

The Deming *system of profound knowledge* provides sound principles upon which the new professionalism can be grounded. Because of the trust issue, this level of change will require more than the simple application of tools and assessments.

Now, let's turn to question 1—how will we measure professionalism? Further, how can we use these metrics to drive higher levels of professional performance?

How can we measure professionalism?

Several articles and books reviewed for this project strongly inferred that professionalism could not be codified into a set of skills or behaviors. Each in their own way, stressed that professionalism was more about *attitude* than behavior. Yet time and again we read about unprofessional *acts*. Of course we can't be sure of what was behind these acts, and certainly attitude is a prime suspect, but to oversimplify something as complex as professionalism into a one dimensional fix of "getting a better professional attitude" did not seem adequate for the challenges at hand.

Put simply, if we value professionalism, we must learn to measure it.

From this perspective, professionalism is little different than other complex behaviors that we have already learned how to codify, observe, train, and measure. These include *leadership, communication,* and *teamwork*. Following this approach, there are four basic requirements for the valid assessment of professionalism:

- *Definitions:* Definitions allow common understanding, which in turn leads to the ability to discriminate between good, better and best. This is where the *variation* element of Deming's *system of profound knowledge* comes into play. Once all elements of professionalism have been defined, the next challenge is creating standards of performance.

- *Standards:* Standards are specific levels of performance based upon the discrete definition of the attribute being measured. Standards must be clearly defined and fixed, not arbitrary or subject to vague interpretation. This requires valid and reliable assessments.

- *Assessments:* Assessment tools should not be so complicated that it takes a Ph.D. to administer or interpret them. All tools designed to evaluate human performance should, at a minimum, have enough room on the scale to evaluate *substandard, meets standards,* and *distinguished* performance levels. This allows data to be turned into actionable recommendations for improvement. All Going Pro assessments have been designed with these goals in mind.

- *Training:* There are actually two types of training that must be accomplished to fully leverage the power of assessment. The first is minimal training on the use and limits of the assessment tool itself. Every tool has its leverage points and weak areas. If you know these in advance, you can optimize the output for more meaningful improvement. The second, and most significant training, is the training of the concepts of the new professionalism itself. Assessment without comprehension of the topic can lead to misinterpretation of results. Like a wise man once said, *a little knowledge can be a dangerous thing.*

All four of these elements were created, tested, and refined during the research and development phase which created the standards of the new professionalism. Starting now, Level III professionalism is observable, measureable, and trainable. Don't be afraid to step on the scale.

The Professionalism Qualifications Rating Scale (PQRS)

Speaking of scales, the following figure is an example of one tool used to train qualified observers how to assess performance with regards to one element of *professional ethics—honesty.*

Meets Standards (1.0)	Distinguished (1.5)	Sub Standard (0)
Tells the truth about all things and actively communicates and reports when required	Sincere and frank in discussions even when expressing unpopular positions; delivers bad news with candor even when to their personal disadvantage	Willing to bend the truth for personal ends; occasionally deceitful; fails to report when required to do so; remains silent when in possession of required information

Example of Behavioral Markers and Scoring Criteria (Honesty) from the Professional Qualifications Rating Scale (PQRS)

The PQRS has created similar behavioral markers for over 150 discrete elements of professionalism. Additional assessments were developed from this list to measure self-perceptions (*GoingPro Quickstart*), values (*Professional Attributes Strength Inventory*), and peer assessments (*GoingPro 360*) of each. Some can be taken online, others are text based, and others are designed to trend professionalism growth over a period of ten years or more (*GoingPro Chronos*).

One size does not fit all. The objective for all of these tools is to provide a variety of means for individuals and organizations to accurately assess and improve across the expansive skill set of the new professionalism from various angles. There is something for everyone at every stage of professional growth.

The next issue to discuss is where to start. Is it best to begin with self-assessment or organizational measures?

Inside out—or outside in?

Those who have read my previous work know that I have a tremendous bias towards self-improvement. Abolitionist Henry Ward Beecher best captures my thoughts in this regard with this quote: "Never excuse yourself (for less than you are capable of). Hold yourself responsible for a higher standard than anybody else expects of you." This leads to a short discussion of our current performance rating systems.

> "In modern organizations, supremely talented people are measured against ridiculously low standards relative to their potential."

In my humble opinion and experience, most employee evaluations are superficial and timid. In modern organizations, supremely talented people are measured against ridiculously low standards relative to their potential. As individuals, we can, and must, raise that bar if we want to get better at what we do and approach our God-given potential. A few words from the *Introduction* of my previous book, *Blue Threat: Why to Err is Inhuman*, captures the need for an inside-out approach to assessing and improving performance as a first step.

> Routine assessment of personal performance is a *discipline*, a body of knowledge and new way of viewing and interacting with the world around you. Once you learn to accurately and objectively see the world through the lens of your individual behaviors and uniqueness (for good and ill), you reach a level of self-awareness and self-assurance unreachable to those without your newly acquired skills. The time it takes you to develop this point of view will come back to you tenfold and more. You will make a new friend and mentor—the one that looks back at you

SETTING THE BAR: THE NEW PROFESSIONALISM

in the mirror each day ... If you choose to reject this approach, I ask only that you make it a conscious choice—and here is the choice clearly spelled out.

> "Far too many choices get made for us by our own indecision."

If you choose to refuse the pain of rigorous personal assessment in the new discipline of *professionalism*, you are hereby agreeing to endure the pain of regret should missed opportunities or avoidable errors lead to unwanted consequence or tragedy. That choice is yours and yours alone.

The reason I want to force this early decision is that far too many choices get made for us by our own indecision. Here is another way of looking at it. If you are not mindful of the dangers posed by avoidable errors and lost opportunities, you can reach a point where you have made unintentional but vitally important choices without thinking, without reflection, without planning, and with no way to reset the chess board. You can end up not having the career you thought you would or living the life you meant to. It might be the one you deserve, but not the one you intended. Or, you have the opportunity to choose a different approach to the rest of your life.[3]

> "When we are all looking for the same attributes, we will discover ground truth."

---

[3] Introduction, *Blue Threat: Why to Err is Inhuman.* Tony Kern, 2009. Pygmy Books.

We can and should <u>initially</u> measure our professionalism from the inside. This can be done with some accuracy with tools designed by professionals to measure *knowledge, behaviors, perceptions, values,* and *attitudes*. But self-perceptions are not enough.

To provide confirmation of our internal perspective, we should also measure professionalism from the outside, with peer reviews, observation tools and by training supervisors and mentors how to observe, recognize, and coach Level III professionalism. In this manner, we immerse ourselves in an environment and culture of professionalism based on shared standards. When we are all looking for the same attributes, we will discover ground truth.

Now we need to look at the system itself and get our heads around the specific elements and standards of the new professionalism.

The science and the system of professionalism

As my colleagues and I set out to discover what a codified system of professionalism might look like, I expected to find several already assembled in whole cloth from which to choose. When the initial scratching of the surface turned up nothing of the sort, I went into my serious research mode and began to look *hard*, combing foreign language research, obscure journals, and the myriads of books on the *pop psychology* and *self-help* shelves at the bookstores. The cupboard was pretty bare.

There are hundreds of references to *professionalism*, but nearly all in reference to its absence or lack thereof. A few, such as *Professionalism:*

Skills for Workplace Success[4] approach the topic from a job finding and career advancement perspective, but limit the discussion to tips and techniques to get and stay on a positive career path. Others, such as *The Power of Professionalism: The Seven Mind-Sets that Drive Performance and Build Trust*[5] take the attitudinal approach of developing new mindsets for enhancing professionalism. Both of these books are easy reads and thoroughly accomplish their objectives. I recommend them both.

Everyone is saying we need more professionalism, but no one was doing the heavy lifting of definitions, standards and assessment that individuals or organizations would need to make the change, or at least make the change *permanent*.

There is a general – and false – assumption that *professionalism* is a commonly understood virtue, yet in our investigations, expert opinions varied widely on what it was, as well as what levels of professionalism one has a right to expect. At this point, We began the effort to define the world's first comprehensive set of professionalism definitions and standards.

The new professionalism

Like all nontechnical skills, the first challenge was finding the existing literature and defining the content into something relevant, learnable, and measureable. I discovered a touchstone in a speech by Air Force General Norton Schwartz, who was trying to get the

---

[4] Anderson, Lydia and Sandra Bolt. *Professionalism: Skills for Workplace Success* 2nd ed. Prentice Hall. 2010.
[5] Wiersma, Bill, and Tony La Russa. *The Power of Professionalism: The Seven Mind-Sets that Drive Performance and Build Trust*. Ravel Media. 2011.

Air Force back on track following a series of embarrassing mistakes, including the unintentional movement of nuclear weapons across the country on a B-52 bomber without anyone knowing it. In one of his first speeches to the troops, General Schwartz said,

"We must do the right thing, and do the right thing right. That is as simple as it gets."[6]

This quote became the essence of the development of the new professionalism. During the course of the research and development effort, we engaged with over 2,500 professionals from a wide variety of career fields in focus groups, interviews with key experts, surveys, and program test and evaluation. By getting their thoughts, inputs and refinements on the program elements, we were able to develop the relative importance, or weight, of each factor. At the time of this writing, the new professionalism program encompasses six domains and nearly 30 subcategories, all with weighting factors, definitions, standards, and observable behaviors.

From here, we took the newly defined professionalism and linked to the proven concept of *deliberate practice*, which is discussed in detail in the next chapter. With the concepts of holistic professionalism defined, ranked, and coupled with a process for evaluation and improvement, the change we desire is at hand.

The figure that follows illustrates the six primary domains of professionalism along with their weighting factors based on their overall importance.

---

[6] http://www.balad.afcent.af.mil/news/story.asp?id=123121227

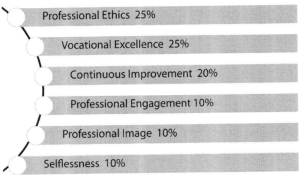

Six Domains of the New Professionalism – Weighted

Said in another way, if, within each of us, there were 100 parts of our professional makeup, 25 of them would be dedicated to "doing the right thing"—*professional ethics.*

Twenty-five more would be used to drive our capability to "do the right thing right" at an expert level from both a technical and nontechnical perspective—*vocational excellence.*

Twenty pieces of *continuous improvement* would fight the natural forces of apathy and complacency and ensure that we continue to grow, and not shrink, as professionals throughout our careers.

Ten pieces of *professional engagement* would keep us focused on the customer, aware of industry best practices, and link us socially to others with whom we can discuss and share our ideas about the future of our respective organizations and industries.

Mix in ten parts of *professional image*—the external indicator of our attention to detail and pride in our profession.

Finally, the entire package is activated with ten pieces of *selflessness*, to keep our egos in check and prevent the progressive disease of careerism from gaining a foothold inside our professionalism fortress.

All manmade interpretations of the natural world are somewhat flawed, and this one is no exception. However, as a guide for personal assessment and professionalism growth, this one (currently) stands alone as the first of its kind.

From here, the task is "making it real," to steal a line from comedian Dave Chappelle. Towards that end, let's dive into our next chapter to discover a proven path to high performance.

"Deliberate practice is hard. It hurts. But it works. More of it equals better performance. Tons of it equals great performance."

Geoff Colvin, Author of
Why Talent is Overrated

Chapter 5

The Deliberate Practice of Professionalism

"There is remarkable potential in 'ordinary' adults and their amazing capacity for change with practice."

K. Anders Ericsson, Professor, psychologist, and framer of the *deliberate practice* concept

THE DELIBERATE PRACTICE OF PROFESSIONALISM 105

The word started to leak out in the early 1990's, but you had to be looking for it to find it.[1] A group of psychologists working on a "universal theory of expertise" discovered a couple of odd things. When they were looking for high achievement indicators, two of their most basic entering assumptions, *experience* and *intelligence*, didn't seem to matter much.

I would have loved to have been a fly on the wall when the stats guy for the team put those findings up in front of his colleagues.[2]

"What have you been smokin' dude?"

"Say what!?!"

---

[1] Camerer, C. and Johnson, E. "The Process-Performance Paradox in Expert Judgment: How Can Experts Know So Much and Predict So Badly?" in K. Anders Ericsson and Jaqui Smith, eds., Toward a General Theory of Expertise: Prospects and Limits (New York: Cambridge University Press, 1991), p. 195-217.

[2] In most research teams, there is one central "data guy" who works the statistical analysis. This avoids any temptation to "tweak the numbers" to prove a hypothesis on the part of a team member. It doesn't always work, but it's a nice cross-check process.

"You better re-run your data man."

The deeper they looked, and the more data they obtained from fields as varied as medicine, sports, chess, music, and others, the more convinced they became that *experience* and *intelligence* were not solid predictors of world-class performance.

Fast forward a decade of serious research and the answers began to emerge. Led by the research of Florida State psychologist K. Anders Ericsson, the researchers began to look hard at the mystery of what creates world-class performance. Slowly but certainly, the secrets of excellence revealed themselves through the data. And it wasn't what anyone thought. Specifically, three traditional wisdoms were challenged and disproven:

- "Innate talent" didn't matter, and perhaps didn't even exist.
- Experience didn't matter, at least in the way we thought it did.
- Intelligence didn't matter, at least not as a limiting factor.

These were hard truths for the world to accept, and to a large extent, Ericsson's findings fell upon deaf ears until two world-class journalists picked up the drumbeat.

In 2008, Malcolm Gladwell published *Outliers: The Story of Success*, and it went to number one on the New York Times non-fiction bestseller list for 11 weeks. Throughout the book, Gladwell—a master storyteller—repeatedly references Ericsson's work, specifically the *10,000 hour rule*, claiming that the key to success in any field is, to a large extent, a matter of deliberately practicing a specific task for a total of around 10,000 hours. *Outliers* drew a lot of us human performance junkies back to the original research, to see how it might apply.

THE DELIBERATE PRACTICE OF PROFESSIONALISM **107**

The second major breakthrough came in two parts. Geoff Colvin, an editor at *Fortune* magazine, wrote an article in the October 19, 2006 edition titled *What it takes to be great*. Following enthusiastic feedback to the article, Colvin followed up with his best seller *Talent is Overrated: What Really Separates World-Class Performers From Everybody Else*. In the book, Colvin lays out the how's and why's of the truly world-class expert, but then struggles to understand why mature professionals and organizations practice these concepts so little. In Chapter 7, he laments,

> We're awed by the performance of a champion sports team or great orchestras and theater companies, but when we get to the office, it occurs to practically no one that we might have something to learn by studying how some people became so accomplished.[3]

After reading Colvin's analysis, former US Army officer Brett Miller picked up on this theme in his online blog:

> To simply say that the Army engages in "deliberate practice"—at both the individual and organizational levels—would be a gross understatement. In fact, in a peacetime Army, the primary activity of soldiers and units is deliberate practice, with the explicit goal of continually improved performance ... When I left the military and joined the corporate world, what struck me most was how little practicing—and how little learning and improving—anyone did. For anything. The general impression was that if you needed to "practice," then you obviously were the wrong person for the job.[4]

---

[3] Colvin, Geoff. *Talent is Overrated: What Really Separates World-Class Performers From Everybody Else*. Portfolio Books. New York. 2008. P. 108.
[4] http://blog.gbrettmiller.com/you-dont-get-better-at-writing-essays-by-writing-more-essays/

Because the world has been slow on the pickup of these revelatory findings, Level III professionals can rapidly distinguish themselves vis-a-vis peers who are most likely not even aware of these concepts.

As we will soon see, the big issues for everyone that contemplates the deliberate practice concept are *time* and *resources*. I took this issue on in *Blue Threat*, where I made the point that even though 10,000 hours is a long time to practice anything, if it can be incorporated into multiple aspects of daily work and life, the goal is achievable in less time than one might initially think. Here is the excerpt that explains the "deliberate practice lifestyle" approach.

> In Malcolm Gladwell's best seller *Outliers*, he explains the *10,000 hour rule*. Evaluating those who have achieved world-class expertise in everything from piano playing and chess to the Beatles and Bill Gates, researchers seem to have discovered that practice does indeed make perfect, or at least *expert*. If, as Gladwell suggests "ten thousand hours is the magic number of greatness," what does that mean for those of us who can't find ten minutes to spare in our action packed lives, let alone 10,000 hours? We will deal with the time question in a moment, but the underlying questions are more important. What could you possibly study or do for 10,000 hours that would not be obsolete by the time you finished? Or a more sobering question. At this stage of your life, if you put 10,000 hours of effort into something, would you be too old to have it make any appreciable difference in your life?
>
> Let's first look at this from the vocational side. Assuming you work the standard 40-hour week and take a couple of weeks' vacation, you work about 2,000 hours per year. Ten thousand hours is five full years of 100% practice on whatever it is you

THE DELIBERATE PRACTICE OF PROFESSIONALISM 109

are trying to become an expert in. Assuming you really can only dedicate 25% of your work on a single practice and you are dedicated to improving each and every day, we are looking at 20 years to become an expert at something under the 10,000 hour rule. Ouch.

If we look at trying to achieve the 10,000 hour goal in the time we have to spend on our hobbies or leisure activities, the picture is even grimmer. Maybe in the next life, eh?

> "In 3-5 years we could accumulate the requisite 10,000 hours of practicing personal excellence and professionalism."

But what if the subject I was trying to become an expert on was *me*? What if, as a routine part of my daily life, I learned to see and analyze my *professionalism* day to day, hour by hour; not as an obsession, but as a routine life skill—a *discipline*? What if I could accumulate 10,000 expert building hours at work, at home, and at play? What would that buy me in terms of performance or competitive edge? How long would it take?

It turns out that most of us are awake and doing things for about 5,700 hours each year. Assuming that we learn to systematically review our daily performance and refine our performance awareness and analysis skills, it is reasonable to assume that in 3-5 years we could accumulate the requisite 10,000 hours of practicing *personal excellence* and *professionalism*. Here is the cool thing. No matter where you go or what you are doing, you are right there doing it. All you need to do is pay attention, close attention, and use the feedback to grow.

By using the world as our classroom and applying the tools to methodically practice excellence *as a life skill and not just a job skill*, we can get an accurate reflection and have justifiable and well-earned confidence. Success and the economic security that comes with it will follow naturally in the wake of this type of expertise.

From an organizational point of view, this idea of dramatic and predictable growth through "practicing within the work" raises the stakes to an entirely new level.

What would happen within our organizations if we could empower our key personnel with tools to systematically improve in the means we have described above? How much of a competitive edge might that be?

> "The deliberate practice of professionalism offers a new approach that leverages the precise environment of the relevant workplace, and does so at a small fraction of the cost."

Organizations spend millions to send their next generation of leaders to expensive business schools and seminars, which are nearly identical in nature and have no way to address the unique conditions of the organization, environment, or individual variances of the high potential leader who attends these executive factories. In this sense, these programs offer very little competitive edge beyond the pedigree of the institution. And we continue to see high potentials derail or burn out at an alarming rate.

The *deliberate practice of professionalism* offers a new approach that leverages the precise environment of the relevant workplace, and does so at a small fraction of the cost. Furthermore, it provides those who fail to get identified and selected for the high-priced programs another option for gaining the fast track.

But you don't have to be a high potential business exec to take advantage of these concepts. They will work anywhere and at any level.

The remainder of this chapter briefly outlines the steps of deliberate practice, juxtaposed against the new standards of professionalism contained in the following six chapters.

"Deliberate practice does require that you consistently push the envelope of your performance, so if you have been on cruise control, this may require an adjustment period, both in terms of attitude and workload."

Let's move on to overview the requirements of the deliberate practice process and see how we might apply them to climbing the ladder to Level III professionalism. In doing so, we will lean heavily on Colvin's interpretation of Ericsson and colleagues to flesh out the remainder of this description.

The elements of deliberate practice

Deliberate practice is a process, but it is not a recipe. Although following the steps will produce highly predictable results, the process does not fall apart if one or more of the steps are not met to the letter. The process merely becomes less effective and will likely take longer. As we walk through each step, don't let the complexity scare you off. Look for areas in your work that lend themselves to immediate application, and fill in the gaps as you begin to work the process. At the final turn of the road, this has to work for you.

In each step, I provide glimpses of what is coming in the next six chapters as we work through the nuts and bolts of the six domains of the new professionalism, but must leave it to you to determine where they fit into your current environment and situation.

1. **Deliberate practice is highly demanding mentally, requiring high levels of focus and concentration.**

   We might lose a few right here, because most experienced professionals have mastered their jobs to the point of being able to do most of it sleepwalking. The real need for added focus and concentration is not to do your job better, but rather to be able to observe yourself against the new professional standards as you do the work. Over time, this becomes a bit less demanding as you become accustomed to the evaluative mindset.

   Deliberate practice does require that you consistently push the envelope of your performance, so if you have been on cruise control, this may require an adjustment period, both in terms of attitude and workload.

2. **It is designed specifically to improve performance—to strengthen it beyond its current levels.**

   You can't just put in time and repetition and expect to get significantly better at anything. You must consistently stretch yourself, and then stretch some more. This relates closely to the concept of "flow" created by Mihaly Csikszenmihalyi, and articulated in his book, *Flow: The Psychology of Optimal Experience*. Csikszenmihalyi describes how nonlinear leaps in performance are often made by high achievers in the "flow channel." When we stretch ourselves in areas of existing competence, we place ourselves in the "flow channel" and give ourselves the best chance to grow quickly. The concept is illustrated in the following figure.

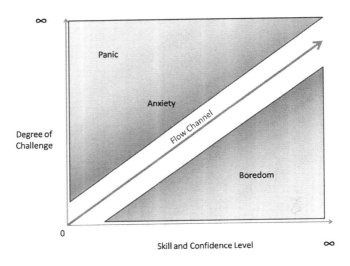

The Flow Channel[5]

If we push our performance envelope and simultaneously keep the balance right between the level of challenge and our maximum level of competence, we can be relatively sure we are following the precepts of deliberate practice.

3. It must continue for long of periods of time.

This is the now famous 10,000 hours/10 years rule.[6] While the researchers suggest that "expert performance levels cannot usually be attained with less than 10 years of continued, vigorous effort" *improvement* can be attained almost immediately upon beginning the process. When we combine this potential with

---

[5] Csikszenmihalyi, Mihaly. *Flow: The Psychology of Optimal Experience*
[6] While early research stressed 10,000 hours of practice, subsequent research expanded it to include the ten year duration, stating them not as averages, but as "minimums" to reach world-class levels of performance.

the "flow channel" concept that suggests leaps of performance are possible if triggered by external demands, we see that professional growth is likely to be nonlinear, and perhaps much faster than we might anticipate. Most of us have experienced "concentrated learning," where certain events crammed years of experience into single episodes.

For me, one of those episodes occurred on December 9, 1983 at exactly 1332 Zulu time, give or take a few seconds. While flying as an Air Force copilot in a KC-135 air refueling tanker over the Persian Gulf, I was involved in a severe mid-air collision with an E-3A AWACs aircraft. The details of the story are interesting, but not all that relevant to our current discussion. For our purposes here, suffice to say that I learned how I respond in a life-threatening emergency. After 11 seconds of metal-on-metal, we found ourselves on fire, nearly inverted, and with two of our four engines inoperative.

For those who have not experienced an event of this type, memories are etched permanently. I can still recall the sounds, smells, sights, and my exact frame of mind as if it happened this morning.

I did not panic, but my brain went into instant *overdrive*. Overdrive doesn't quite capture what was happening in my head; perhaps *warp speed* describes it better. Instantaneously, I had a rush of information fire across my synapses: *two engine out procedures, minimum airspeeds with no right hydraulic system, controllability check procedures, AC electrical load limits for single generator operations, ...* Had you quizzed me prior to takeoff on any of these items, I would have been hard pressed to tell you where to find them in the manuals, let alone spit them out verbatim without reference.

Of course the rest of my crew had no idea what all the gibberish I was spouting out had to do with anything, and I had to force myself back into a common time equilibrium to be of any value to the situation. To make a long story short, we made it back onto a Saudi Arabian runway with a wonderful crew effort, but what I learned about myself in those 39 minutes has shaped the way I have approached the world ever since. Specifically,

- Study matters. I worked hard in my initial qualification courses to master the knowledge of my aircraft. When it mattered, the information was there for me.

- I don't panic under extreme conditions, but I have to force myself to slow down or I will get out of sync with the rest of the team, quite possibly making matters worse.

- I learned that things can go from green to mean in a nanosecond. One moment you are ops normal, the next you are upside down and on fire. My vigilance has been forever heightened. I <u>know</u> it can happen to me.

- Finally, I view each minute on this side of the event as a gift. There is an old proverb that says, *those who live on borrowed time, live on trespass ground.* I try my best to make my days count.

I can state with some certainty that those 39 minutes had more learning packed into them than the rest of my flying years combined. I don't know if I was in the flow channel, but I am certain that when preparation meets opportunity, speed learning is possible.

What this means for us, is that the sooner we get started, and the more we challenge ourselves, the faster we have the potential to grow. If we get lucky enough to experience (and survive) a few concentrated learning experiences, so much the better.

4. **It must be repeated, and adjustments made during the repetitions.**

One of K. Anders Ericsson's first findings was that repetition alone won't get you to world-class levels of excellence. Colvin explains that the repetition must be in "the learning zone," by which he means sufficiently challenging and measured. For example, a golf duffer like me might go out and hit 100 golf balls on the driving range, whereas a professional would hit the same 100 balls with the goal of getting 85% of them within 15 feet of the target pole. Using the same example, I might daydream while practicing, but the pro would be constantly monitoring multiple aspects of his swing and adjusting throughout to get more accuracy.

Let's take this off the driving range and into our professional environments. One example might be a "duffer" pilot who logs 500 safe flying hours, but without pushing himself or measuring against a higher standard of professionalism, really is logging one hour five-hundred times. Conversely, a Level III professional pilot practices precision, monitors and adjusts throughout, and actually achieves more learning in 25 hours of deliberate practice than his peer who logged 20 times more flying time than he did but failed to push himself to learn the lessons that were available.

THE DELIBERATE PRACTICE OF PROFESSIONALISM 117

5. It requires continuous feedback on results.

The research tells us that this is the area where having a great teacher, coach, or mentor can make all the difference. With the new professionalism standards, it is unlikely that anyone will be further advanced than you are when you finish this book. So for the time being, we must be our own coach, unless we can find a peer or two to begin the journey with. What *is* clear is that those who make the effort *now* will be in an excellent position to become a great coach and mentor to those who follow.

Throughout the next six chapters, we will provide specific actionable benchmarks to help with the critical feedback equation.

6. Pre-performance preparation is essential.

My mid-air collision is an excellent example of this. This is where goal-setting comes in—you have to know what you need to know and where you want to go if you expect to get there. As Ericsson, Gladwell, and Colvin all point out, goal-setting "should involve not merely outcomes, but also the processes involved in reaching predetermined goals." For process purposes, I like planning forms and checklists, mostly because I am old school and these tools don't rely on electrons flowing in any particular direction.

In *Blue Threat*, we included the *Blue Threat Report and Analysis Tool* (BRAT)[7] which was specifically designed for the process of personal error identification and analysis. Similarly,

---

[7] Kern, Tony. *Blue Threat: Why to Err is Inhuman.* Pygmy Books. Colorado Springs. 2009. p. 237-239.

performance metrics and process tools are available for benchmarking against the new professionalism standards, many contained in the next six chapters.

7. **Deliberate practice involves self-observation and self-reflection.**

    We addressed this pretty well in the first paragraph on why deliberate practice is so mentally demanding. The bottom line here is <u>as</u> you practice, you need to be continually aware of your own performance and be focused on correcting and adapting on the fly. This kind of in-the-moment self-assessment is critical and just takes time to develop. The more you do it, the easier it gets, until it becomes second nature and nearly automatic.

8. **It involves careful reflection on performance after practice sessions are completed.**

    Attention is a limited resource, and there is only so much in-the-moment assessment one can do, especially if you are truly challenging yourself "in the learning zone." In addition to being aware of your performance as you are practicing, you need to look back on it with finer discrimination once you are done and determine where you might have improved. This is also the time to set your new stretch goals.

    For example, a contract negotiation team finishes a high-stakes marathon negotiation that results in huge success and new business for their company. Before the second cigar (or the first drink), take the time for a personal after action review while the memories and details are still fresh in your mind. More lessons are lost following successful outcomes by failing to do this than in any other manner.

These are the essential steps of deliberate practice. In reviewing the research again in preparation for writing this chapter, one item stood out. In the final analysis, it seems that experience <u>does</u> matter, but only a certain type of experience; *structured experience that was specifically designed to improve and that was practiced in a very specific manner.*

Colvin believes that the discipline of deliberate practice evolves into a new mindset, and that

> Armed with that mindset, people go at a job in a new way. Research shows they process information more deeply and retain it longer. They want more information on what they're doing and seek other perspectives. They adopt a longer-term point of view. In the activity itself, the mindset persists. You aren't just doing the job, you're explicitly trying to get better at it in the larger sense.[8]

There are no accidental experts. World-class athletes have a mantra they use to move from a perception of adequacy to the next performance level. It goes like this: *Good—Better—Great—Best—How?* "I'm good, need to be better, want to be great, might someday be the best; how do I do it?" The tasks of deliberate practice are neither intuitive nor easy. If they were, everyone would do it. The path is now available, but the willful choice to follow that path is what will separate Level III professionals from their peers.

One last important point is that the road to excellence through deliberate practice starts steep, but becomes much, much easier when the results begin to appear.

---

[8] Colvin, Geoff. "Why Talent is Overrated." Fortune Magazine online article. Found at http://money.cnn.com/2008/10/21/magazines/fortune/talent_colvin.fortune/index2.htm

Blue Threat Proverb 17[9] states it best in this manner:

Self-improvement defies gravity

> *There comes a point in every improvement effort where we begin to see the results of our efforts. From that point forward, what was once an uphill climb—laborious effort for no apparent gain—becomes worth the time and effort, and eventually effortless and nearly automatic behavior. Race car driver Danica Patrick explains her early success this way, "I really had this obsession to keep getting better. I got hooked on the improvement, and the gains that can be made, and the satisfaction that comes from it." This crucial point—the apex of the improvement effort where gains become apparent—is where permanent change becomes a serious reality. Manage this correctly, and you will achieve the "normalization of excellence" where further improvement fuels itself.*

Now it is on to the specifics of the six domains of the new professionalism.

On deck—*professional ethics.*

---

[9] The Blue Threat Proverbs are a series of 31 insights on self-improvement contained in chapter 12 of Blue Threat, p. 214-235. They are also available as a full color poster set from Convergent Performance at http://www.convergentperformance.com

"Relativity applies to physics, not ethics."

Albert Einstein

Chapter 6

The Ethics of Professionalism

"In the land of the blind, the one-eyed man is king."
In regione caecorum rex est luscus.

Desiderius Erasmus, Dutch philosopher

THE ETHICS OF PROFESSIONALISM

*P*rofessional *ethics* is a deceptively complex issue. It is personal, volatile, and potentially a legal powder keg. It makes people nervous. This is true largely because any discussion of ethics involves questioning another's *morality*. So let's start this crucial discussion with a simple question: *How important is morality to a professional?*

At its core, professional ethics is about one thing—*trust*. Trust between an organization and its workers; trust between employees and their leaders; trust between a service provider and their customers; trust between peers; and trust between the better and lesser angels of your own conscience.

Just as professional ethics is the cornerstone of trust, trust is the one essential ingredient in *culture*. Nearly everyone recognizes the importance of culture, and discussions, plans, and programs about how to improve cultures are routine. So why is it easier to talk about culture (which is based upon trust, which is created by ethical conduct) but far more difficult to talk about ethics itself?

Culture is organizational. It's about groups and is sufficiently vague and fuzzy enough not to threaten our personal self-esteem. Ethics is none of these things. It is personal and necessarily judgmental. Unlike culture, ethics is not about *us*, it is about *me*. It looks deep.

Almost by definition, ethics involves a person's faith, parenting, motivations, ambition, values and self-perception of all the aforementioned. Each of these areas is explosive in its own right, but reaches critical mass when mixed together inside of a real person and then subjected to the challenges of the day to day workplace and the light of outside scrutiny. Talking—or even thinking—about one's own professional ethics can be uncomfortable at best, especially if there are some less than perfect things hidden under the rocks. And don't we all have a few of those?

Unfortunately, this leads many who make their living researching and talking about ethics to frame the discussion in a timid, third-person manner. They may be willing to talk about professional ethics in general, but not their personal ethics or your personal ethics. That sort of academic cowardice does little for anyone seeking to be a Level III professional. The issue of ethics is so important, so critical to authentic professionalism, that we must take it to task. When I say we, I mean you and I as individuals taking a hard look, not some soft, gooey organizational version of professional ethics.

So for the remainder of this chapter, I will not shirk from asking you to question and examine your own personal ethics and value systems, beginning with the assumption that they could be improved. I know mine certainly can.

Let's begin with untangling a few of the major elements of professional ethics and ask ourselves how we rate against some tough standards. Then, we can lower the temperature to see if we can reach a point where we have a common set of agreed upon benchmarks.

Morphing right vs. wrong into right vs. right

To do the right thing, we have to know what *right* is. In a secular society like ours, everyone is entitled to their own definitions, so long as they stay on the right side of the law. Since the founding of the first democratic secular society, this has led to serious challenges when one attempts to draw a clean line between right and wrong. In nearly any *rightness* decision, questions arise that muddy the water in even the most basic of right vs. wrong decisions.

- Right for whom? Is my best course of action based upon what is right for me, or what is right for others? Many find ways to rationalize that what is right for me will always be right for others. For example, "if I lie and cheat to get the next promotion, is that not justifiable based upon my ability to take better care of my family or give more to my favorite charity?"

- Right for when? If I take this noncompliant shortcut now, it may allow me to do the right thing later when it will be more important. We see this all the time in job- and task-related decisions. For example, if a maintenance technician is faced with using a non-approved replacement part in a repair that is not strictly "by the book" but good enough to get the job done, are they doing their boss a favor?

- Loyalty vs. honesty. If I tell the truth about an unethical or noncompliant act by a friend or coworker, they may be punished or perhaps even fired if management finds out. This ethical issue often rises in many organized labor vs. management negotiations, where both sides have been known to deceive and do less than their best to apply more pressure to the other.

- "Outsourced ethics." When these types of decisions are made in a group setting, the ethical considerations are often "outsourced" to the group or cultural norm. For example, if we stay with the labor vs. management example, and a strategy of a "work slowdown" is determined to be the most effective means of pressuring management, the employee who takes part in the activity must make a determination between his or her personal code that says "I will do my best every day," and the "outsourced" ethics of their union. Likewise, some cultures that favor getting the job done no matter what it takes will strongly impose its cultural norms on those who might otherwise act more responsibly.

The common element in these and many other ethical dilemmas is that they create mental conditions where the softer road is rationalized as for the so-called "greater good." Compounding this ethical smog is a philosophical school of thought called *situational ethics* that argues every decision must be analyzed in terms of its own context, which opens up a Pandora's box of "if it feels good at the time, do it" options.

While we can all agree that all situations are unique and pose different challenges for decision makers, professional ethics is so foundational to holistic professionalism that we can't afford to go too far down the slippery slope of situational ethics. In the real world, professionals need standards to guide their decisions and assist them in making the hard calls.

Is cheating a competitive edge?

One of the biggest problems is that lying and cheating is seen by some as a competitive edge, and it often works, at least in the short term. A second major issue is that while *ethics* is one of those areas we seldom discuss, reward, or punish, *success* is nearly the polar opposite. We are a results driven society and pay homage to the winners.

If lying and cheating are the unstated "rules of the game" in some business or political circles, can an honest man or woman even compete? The short answer is "yes" but only if they have a set of guiding principles and are willing to stick with them.

Let's face facts; many in our society have been known to look the other way if the results are favorable. It might be something as simple as backdating paperwork to pass an inspection or fudging a few numbers on a PowerPoint slide to enhance a quarterly report. Or, it could be something far more systemic. Once on the path, it is extremely difficult to reclaim the lost virtue of ethical conduct. It is much easier to *preserve* virtue than to *reclaim* it.

Let's take a look at marginalized ethics in action and how it played out in the largest public school cheating scandal in America's history; only this time it wasn't the students who were caught cheating.

The Atlanta Public School cheating scandal: A case study of systemic ethical destruction

In the fall of 2005, Heather Vogell, an investigative reporter at the *Atlanta Journal Constitution*, sat down to analyze some statistics on student performance for an article she was working on. What she saw puzzled her.[1] After reviewing the statistical analysis, she found something that seemed odd. A few schools had increased their performance dramatically more than expected. She began to wonder if someone was tampering with the test results or process. She published her first story in December 2008, highlighting schools where the gains seemed too good to be true.

Three years later, the answers to Ms. Vogell's questions made national news when a state investigation found widespread cheating. In the initial report, at least 178 teachers and principals were found to have routinely erased and corrected incorrect answers on standardized tests. The cheating inflated the scores of thousands of students, giving the false impression of their—and Atlanta Public Schools'—success.

This news shocked the entire education industry, as the Atlanta school system had been recognized as a poster child for urban school improvement. To add insult to injury, the APS Superintendent, Dr. Beverly Hall, had been awarded hundreds of thousands of dollars in bonus pay for her stellar leadership and won a National Superintendent of the Year award for Atlanta's meteoric rise. Ironically, Dr. Hall retired shortly before the state commission report.

Here are a few of the highlights from the state inquiry:

---

[1] Contrary to popular belief, most discoveries do not begin with an "ah-ha" flash of insight, but rather when a curious person with a good mind looks at something and says "that's funny, I wonder why ..." Heather Vogell's curiosity, courage, and dogged determination set a new and positive course for future generations of Atlanta's children.

- "We were confronted by a pattern of interference by top APS leadership in our attempt to gather evidence," investigators wrote. "These actions delayed the completion of this inquiry and hindered the truth-seeking process."
- The report revealed teachers were publicly humiliated or fired for perceived underperformance, and whistleblowers faced more ridicule than cheaters.
- A group of teachers at Gideons Elementary School held a weekend "changing party" at a teacher's home, where they systematically altered test answers to boost results.
- The report describes the case of Michael Milstead, who, upon beginning his tenure as principal of the Harper Archer Middle School, noticed an incredible gap between students' elementary school scores and the scores they were achieving at his school. After he raised the issue of inflated scores at a May 2008 meeting, an education official confronted him, and he was soon told his services were no longer needed.

"In sum, a culture of fear, intimidation, and retaliation permeated the APS system from the highest ranks down," the report concludes.

So what can we learn from this sad affair? For one, we see that any organization that puts *results* ahead of everything else is at risk. There is little doubt that many of these administrators and teachers had rationalized that the accolades and federal funding attached to the falsified test scores were for the "greater good." Several responses to this scandal blamed the federal government (they are always an easy target for shifting blame) for requiring the testing in the first place.

How do we reach a point where <u>hundreds</u> of so called "professional" teachers and administrators are systematically convinced to alter national test scores? Think about the magnitude of this for just a moment. After pouring over the report's testimony, I think that the ethical compromises in this event—and many others like it—went down something like this.

1. The leaders of the ethical compromise demonized existing guidelines as somehow wrong or out of touch. In this manner, they change a clear "right vs. wrong" decision (to cheat or not to cheat) into a "value-based" choice with no clear right or wrong (what is in our best interest). In the case of the Atlanta teacher cheating scandal, many were led to believe that the real evil was the testing itself, and that by circumventing the testing (through blatant answer changing), they could thumb their nose (or extend their middle finger) at President Bush and the "No Child Left Behind" Act testing program.

2. Next, the ethical compromisers showed the advantages of the unethical act. In this case, by altering the test scores they could gain acclaim and economic advantages for themselves, their school, and possibly even their students. They convinced themselves and each other that they were doing this "for the children." The rationalization was that perhaps these children were not learning like they should, but with the government funds that could be had by cheating, future generations might.

3. Once the cheating was widespread, the organization played the "you are either with us or against us" card. When they ran into teachers or administrators who saw the ethical corruption for what it was and refused to go along, they ratcheted up the coercive tactics or quickly removed them from their positions to continue the unethical acts.

THE ETHICS OF PROFESSIONALISM

4. Once the unethical acts were well-established, they institutionalized it with the "cultural norm" card by sharing the fact that others in positions of respect are doing it. "This is not as bad as it sounds and you won't be alone here."

In this manner, the Atlanta Public Schools created cultural norms of cheating, intimidation, and corruption, all while operating under the radar for years. Personal ethical compromise often follows the same pattern.

Interestingly, the establishment—or in some cases re-establishment—of an ethical culture (personal or organizational) works in much the same way, albeit with a different take on a few key topics like *honesty, integrity, loyalty,* and the *rule of law*.

If you find yourself trying to exist within or reverse an ethically challenged culture, try articulating these concepts to yourself and if necessary, to your peers and supervisors in an attempt to hold the line under difficult temptations:

1. Don't be afraid to say "Don't we believe in the rule of law here? We may not like the existing guidelines, but we are legally and duty bound to follow and enforce them. We can strive to change the rules, but in the meantime, we work inside the lines."

2. Show both the short term and long term advantages of ethical conduct as well as the potentially severe disadvantages of *unethical conduct*.

    a. Short term – solid ethics means you won't get caught on the wrong side of the law or public opinion. Note that this requires a *quality assurance* component to hold people at risk for unethical acts, as well as the willpower to act when someone is caught.

b. Create positive incentives for ethical conduct. Catch yourself or someone else doing something positive, and make a note to mention it to them as well as to their peers. A pat on the back or a "well done" goes a long way, even further if you can use the observation in a write up for a cash award or other incentive.

c. Long term – grow a very solid culture that has ethics as a core element of strategy, evaluations, training, and communications.

3. Finally, to the maximum extent possible, be consistent and transparent about how you deal with an unethical act. Let everyone know where you stand and you are less likely to make the first false step down the slippery slope of context-based situational ethics.

Remember, the trick to creating the culture that resulted in the mass cheating scandal in Atlanta was to make what was clearly an unethical act (cheating) into something that looked like an ethical goal (for the kids). When it comes to ethics, this type of "ends justifies the means" approach must be recognized and fought early and often.

Are professional ethics in an irreversible decline?

Many believe that we are going to have to learn to live with ethical compromise. They point out that all the trends in society seem to indicate that the future will be a very gray area. In *Blue Threat*, I

THE ETHICS OF PROFESSIONALISM **135**

spent an entire chapter on "The Myth of Compliance" and posed a few tough questions with sufficient data to suggest we might be in for a rough ride over the next few decades.

- What if from an early age, children were taught that rule breaking, lying, and cheating were acceptable competitive options?
- What if high-achieving children learned early on that some rules were often unfair or unjust, and that they could make their own if they wanted to?
- What if our secular value system made rule breaking a part of daily life?

When the Josephson Institute of Ethics released its 2010 Report Card on the Ethics of American Youth,[2] the evidence was clear that some of our basic beliefs about rule breaking are <u>way</u> off the mark. The survey of over 43,000 high school students nationwide found that over 60% had cheated on a test in the past year and 38% had cheated more than once. So what? Lots of kids cheat in school. What does that have to do with rule breaking by adults at home or in the workplace? Let's look a bit deeper at some issues with clear implications for future workplace behaviors. The following data is taken from the Josephson Institute's *2010 Ethics' Report Card on American Youth's Values and Actions:*[3]

> While 89% of students believe that being a good person is more important than being rich, almost one in three boys and one in four girls admitted stealing from a store within the past year.

---

[2] Following a benchmark survey in 1992, Josephson Institute has conducted a national survey of the ethics of American youth every two years. Data is gathered through a national sample of public and private high schools.

[3] http://charactercounts.org/programs/reportcard/2010/installment02_report-card_honesty-integrity.html

Moreover, 21% admitted they stole something from a parent or other relative, and 18% admitted stealing from a friend.

On lying, more than two in five said they sometimes lie to save money (48% of males and 35% of females).

Rampant cheating in school continues. A majority of students (59%) admitted cheating on a test during the last year, with 34% doing it more than two times. One in three admitted they used the Internet to plagiarize an assignment.

"As bad as these numbers are, they appear to be understated," said Michael Josephson, president of the Institute and a national leader in ethics training. "More than one in four students confessed they lied on at least one or two survey questions, which is typically an attempt to conceal misconduct."

The data from the Josephson Institute have shown a progressive decline in ethical behavior and beliefs in American teens over the past decade.

In his book *Winners Never Cheat*, former Utah Governor and Presidential candidate Jon Huntsman argues that we need to take the issue of "shared values" much more seriously today than in any time in our history. He says this is especially true as we bridge the chasm between the classroom and the boardroom. "Values provide us with ethical water wings whose deployment are as critical in today's wave tossed corporate boardrooms as they were in yesterday's classroom."[4]

---

[4] Huntsman, Jon. *Winners Never Cheat: Even in Difficult* Times. Wharton School Pub. (2008) p. 37

Colleen Carroll Campbell, an author, columnist, and former presidential speechwriter, believes the cause is self-centeredness and that it may impact entire generations of current and future adults. She thinks she knows why we are seeing these problems.

> It's significant that young Americans vulnerable to narcissism were raised in the heyday of the self-esteem movement, when well-meaning baby boomer parents, teachers, and media gurus incessantly urged them to "love yourself first," "let nothing come between you and your dreams," and believe that "you're the best." Rather than stoking healthy self-confidence, such messages may have dampened work ethic while fueling unrealistic expectations and inflated egos. Neither is much use in the real world, where believing in yourself cannot guarantee success and putting your own immediate desires ahead of all other concerns can be a recipe for disaster in work, love, and life.[5]

Psychologists Jean Twenge and W. Keith Campbell, the authors of *The Narcissism Epidemic: Living in the Age of Entitlement*, believe we live in an age of "corrosive narcissism" where indulgent vanity feeds a wide variety of our social ills, not the least of which is rampant noncompliance and rule breaking.

> Today, ever-growing numbers of individuals feel fewer and fewer inner restraints or inhibitions against obeying any law or moral code that interferes with their private desires or impulses. As the social stigma that were once attached to lawbreaking and deviation from traditional morals grow weaker, the distinction between liberty and license becomes more and more blurred

---

[5] Challenging America's me-first culture, by Coleen Carol Campbell, found at http://www.stltoday.com/stltoday/news/columnists.nsf/colleencarrollcampbell/story/A384AD3DCB07FEB2862575AE00810E3E?OpenDocument

in the minds of the individual. Pleasure and profit become the only guides to personal conduct. The law is seen as the enemy to be destroyed or outwitted. In the end, the only sin is getting caught.[6]

Does all of this mean that the problem of poor ethics is simply a part of our societal norms and that we just need to get used to it? Has the process of ethical compromise become irreversible? Or does it represent an opportunity to establish our professional ethical bar far above the crowd and turn it into a competitive edge?

Guerilla warfare: Establishing and maintaining a professional conscience

Society's ethical decline may have a silver lining for Level III professionals. The oft quoted proverb "that in the land of the blind, the one eyed man is King," illustrates that the tables may be turning on those who believe that poor ethics are a competitive advantage.

In Dr. Jerry White's great book, *Honesty, Morality and Conscience*, he juxtaposes two historical examples of the human conscience at work. The first comes courtesy of a story told by Mark Twain and represents those who feel that cheating to get ahead is worth the risk.

> When I was a boy, I was walking along a street and happened to spy a cart full of watermelons. I was fond of watermelon, so I sneaked quietly up to the cart and snitched one. Then I ran to a nearby alley and sunk me teeth into the melon. No sooner

---

[6] Clare Boothe Luce, *US News and World Report*, July 5, 1976 p. 65-66 as quoted in Jerry White's *Honesty, Morality and Conscience*, NavPress. 1979. P. 16.

> had I done so, however, than a strange feeling came over me. Without a moment's hesitation, I made my decision. I walked back to the cart, replaced the melon, and took a ripe one.[7]

A second historical example puts this into perspective and illustrates how an ethical center elevates a person in the eyes of his peers and colleagues.

> When baseball great Ted Williams was 40 years old and closing out his career with the Boston Red Sox, he was suffering from a pinched nerve in his neck. For the first time in his career, he batted under .300, hitting just .254 with 10 home runs. He was the highest salaried player in sports that year, making $125,000. The next year, the Red Sox sent him the same contract. "When I got it," Williams said, "I sent it back with a note that I would not sign it until I received the full pay cut allowed (25%)."

Ted Williams cut his own contract by $31,250, back when that was a LOT of money. Why on earth would anyone do that? When asked, Williams did not hesitate, "My feeling was that I was always treated fairly by the Red Sox … they were offering me a contract I didn't deserve." Williams' reputation for honesty and integrity spread and resulted in numerous advertising and consulting contracts worth far more than the dollars sacrificed. He also slept with a clear conscience, and no price tag can be placed upon that.

These two examples illustrate the one key to overcoming the apparent avalanche of ethical decline—our professional conscience. While the world may have lost its ethical guideposts into a "gray fog of inconsistent moral choices,"[8] the individual remains empowered to chart his or her personal ethical course.

---

[7] Jerry White. *Honesty, Morality and Conscience*, NavPress. 1979. P. 15.
[8] Jerry White. *Honesty, Morality and Conscience*, NavPress. 1979. P. 14.

In a world gone blind to ethical conduct, this may well be a high road to competitive advantage. To work towards this goal, here are a few tools to get on track or improve your ethical game.

Roadblocks, on ramps and fast lanes to improving your professional ethics

The tools provided are designed to re-establish boundaries for our personal professional health. As we start down the path into the six domains of Level III professionalism, we begin each domain with a short assessment. Each of the following five chapters will have similar assessments to the one you are about to complete. Use them to evaluate your current level of professionalism in each area. These short assessments will enhance your awareness of key elements of structured professionalism and provide you with an internal snapshot of your current state. While self-perceptions are valuable to improve self-awareness, the research on their validity indicates they can be well off the mark in some individuals.[9]

It is strongly recommended that those interested in a more in depth assessment with greater validity take the *Professional Attributes Strength Inventory* (PASI) as well as the *GoingPro Chronos* and *Professionalism 360* tools, available through *Corvirtus, LLC*, a visionary company located in Colorado Springs that specializes in valid psychological testing and evaluation. These tools will allow you to accurately assess not only your current state of professionalism development, but also measure your growth over an entire career.

---

[9] Dunning, David; Kerri Johnson, Joyce Ehrlinger; and Justin Kruger (2003). "Why people fail to recognize their own incompetence." *Current Directions in Psychological Science* 12 (3): 83–87.

To get the most out of this tool, it is critical that you are honest with yourself. If in doubt on any statement, score yourself to a lower level to facilitate maximum improvement and stimulate professional growth.

For each of the following questions, grade yourself by circling 0, .5, or 1 in accordance with the following criteria.

0	.5	1
Almost Never	**Sometimes**	**Nearly Always**

Professional ethics is fully 25% of the professionalism equation. Answer the following questions and see where you might have some work to do.

Professional Ethics Self Perceptions

I tell the truth about all things and never withhold important information.

0   .5   1

I report events and deviations when required to, even when they would negatively reflect upon my performance.

0   .5   1

I honor my word whenever I commit to a course of action, i.e., returning calls and emails or completing other follow up actions in a timely manner.

0   .5   1

I follow policies, procedures, and other written or verbal guidance without exception.

<pre>
      0   .5   1
</pre>

I always give my employer or customer respect and "an honest day's work."

<pre>
      0   .5   1
</pre>

SUBTOTAL _____ x 5 = _____ (transfer this weighted score to scorecard at the end of the book)

Calculate the total score and transfer it to the overall professionalism scorecard at the end of the book. This will provide a starting reference point for your journey to Level III professionalism as it relates to professional ethics.

Now, use the following personal inventory to identify roadblocks, find starting points, or to accelerate areas where you are already strong.

Professional Ethics Inventory – *Doing the <u>right</u> thing.*

Although most organizations and industries have a Code of Ethics, we must never forget that organizations don't make decisions—individual human beings do. One of the first steps towards a shared understanding of core professionalism is to ensure we have knowledge and action steps available in four critical elements of ethical conduct; *honesty, integrity, loyalty,* and *accountability.*

Professional Ethics Sub-domain 1. Honesty

Few will argue that honesty is a cornerstone of ethical conduct. Here are a few guidelines for improvement.

Roadblocks

- "No one needs to know" attitude corrupts honesty for personal ends.
- "White lies" of little apparent consequence are made for personal convenience.
- Fear of getting in trouble or being viewed as "a snitch" leads to failure to report when required or when you have helpful information.

On ramps

- Tell the truth about all things big and small.
- Actively communicate and report when required by moving information into the open.
- Be sincere and frank in discussions even when expressing unpopular positions.

Fast lanes

- Practice radical honesty. No white lies, no withheld information, just truth.
- Deliver bad news with candor even when it is difficult and to your personal disadvantage.
- When someone else is being deceitful, tactfully and respectfully reveal the truth if possible.

A second essential to professional ethics is a similar concept, but angled just a bit more on closing the gap between word and deed.

Professional Ethics Sub-domain 2. Integrity

If *honesty* is telling the truth, *integrity* is staying true to your word and your principles.

Roadblocks

- "Situational" ethics drive actions, and personal interests create a sliding scale of ethical behavior.
- People are used and discarded after they no longer add advantage to your personal agenda.
- "Empty" promises are made and not kept to avoid conflict, uncomfortable moments, or for personal advantage.

On ramps

- Become a "person of your word." Keep promises, big and small.
- Show consistency between word and deed in good times and bad.
- Judge behaviors and actions not directly observable by others by asking "would this be considered appropriate by my peers, supervisors, or my *mom*?"

Fast lanes

- Make your handshake as binding as any legal contract.
- Seek opportunities to mentor others in the practice of integrity by proactively using everyday examples to discuss and promote consistency between word and deed.

- Practice "radical follow through" on commitments, even to those whom you have never met (i.e., customers, virtual contacts, etc.).

Integrity to commitments and principles leads us nicely into the next sub-domain of professional ethics, *loyalty*.

Professional Ethics Sub-domain 3. Loyalty

Loyalty can be defined as faithfulness or a devotion to a person, organization, or cause. Use the following tips and tools to help develop this important part of the professional ethics package.

Roadblocks

- Personal agenda drives actions; shortcuts are frequently taken for personal convenience.
- Allegiance to self overrides loyalty to peers or organization.
- Participates in disparaging communications or "gossip" about organization, management, or peers.

On ramps

- Give your employer or customer due respect and "an honest day's work."
- Be consistently loyal to both people and principles.
- Show up on time, all the time, for work and appointments.

Fast lanes

- Go above and beyond what is required to support others not only when it is easy and convenient, but when it is hard and inconvenient.

- Remain steadfastly loyal to others even when it is difficult and disadvantageous to you personally.

Now it's time to move on to the final sub-domain of professional ethics, *accountability*.

Professional Ethics Sub-domain 4. Accountability

Accountability is the *willful* assumption and acceptance of responsibility for all actions and decisions. A key word in this definition is willful, as many organizations and laws attempt to "hold people accountable" through punishment. This is a failed strategy as ethical accountability must be self-imposed to close the loop on decisions as well as actions. Use the following to gain traction in this final and critical aspect of professional ethics.

Roadblocks

- Excuse making for poor outcomes.
- Blames others or external circumstances for things that were or are within your control.
- "Silent lies," withholds information that would be useful to others but personally detrimental.

On ramps

- Hold yourself accountable for measurable high-quality, timely, and cost-effective results.
- Accept responsibility for mistakes and outcomes when appropriate.

- Practice accountability for errors even when they don't result in a bad outcome; i.e., "It came out OK but I could have and should have done better."

Fast lanes

- Invoke the motto of "the buck stops here" and make a habit of taking responsibility and control of actions and attitudes that result in unwanted outcomes.
- Accept <u>some</u> personal responsibility for outcomes even when they were largely influenced by things outside of your control.
- Steadfastly refuse to blame others in any public setting.

Remember, <u>accountability</u> closes the loop on the previous aspects of professional ethics, and for that reason, might be the most critical skill to continuously keep in your crosscheck.

Summary and wrap up on professional ethics

Professional ethics is where the journey to Level III professionalism begins, but we have a long way yet to go. The next step on the journey to Level III professionalism is *vocational excellence*—job skills. The link between ethics and vocational excellence is direct and critical. To paraphrase Sam Johnson and many others, ethics without knowledge and skill is useless but relatively harmless; but knowledge and skill without ethics is downright dangerous.

"We must do the right thing, and do the right thing right. That is as simple as it gets."

General Norton Schwartz,
United States Air Force

Chapter 7

Vocational Excellence (Job Skills): There is No Substitute for Talent

"Let the path be open to talent."
Napoleon Bonaparte

There is no substitute for talent.

Hall of Fame basketball coach (UCLA) and leadership guru John Wooden was once asked how he could keep winning when he lost so many players each year to graduation. He responded, "I'd rather have a lot of talent and a little experience than a lot of experience and a little talent." When you are competing at high levels, there are many components that work together to create conditions for victory, but you simply can't compete on the world stage without talent.

In this chapter, we will look closely at what talent looks like to a Level III professional. In one sense, this is the most difficult chapter in the book to write, as its intent is to make the current notion of "job skills" obsolete; to make it more about holistic professionalism without undermining the critical importance of specific vocational tasks. But before we can do so, we must look at vocational excellence through the lens we have currently available to us. Therefore, we will look at how to broaden our professionalism point of view while simultaneously zeroing in on how we can each identify and calibrate those *specific* skills that are critical to our current occupation or vocation.

There is not enough paper from all the pulp mills in Idaho to identify and evaluate all the specific vocational skills for any particular industry in a book of this general nature, but we can define some core competencies and methods.

There are six broad sub-domains of vocational excellence we will analyze: *Technical credibility, personal discipline and compliance, attention to detail, diligence, nontechnical excellence,* and *problem solving*. In each, we will drill into some specifics and pose questions that will allow each of us to apply these general concepts to our chosen profession.

But before we do, let's embark on a short discussion of how to identify specific competencies and skill levels in any specialty or vocation. The first place to look for these is within the professional standards that already exist.

Where to look

Most vocations have entry level and advanced qualifications standards that are mandated by either the government or an industry association with great credibility. To use an example from professional aviation, we would initially find that to become a money-earning pilot, you must meet some rigorous standards to gain a government *commercial pilot certificate*. This requires an individual to pass detailed theoretical knowledge examinations on such topics as weather and aerodynamics, and also a set of practical examinations on specific Federal Aviation Regulations (FARs) on how aircraft are operated in U.S. airspace. Like with nearly all government examinations, you can either download or purchase detailed study guides to prepare for these examinations, or attend a concentrated "short course" put on by industry specialists.

Fire fighting, law enforcement, and other similar first responder vocations all typically have a set of national approved standards, whereas industries like real estate and the legal profession vary significantly from state to state.

Other high end occupations such as medicine or nuclear technology are unique in that they have a defined set of standards, but approvals are often controlled by industry <u>and</u> government through an agreement where the government grants approval authority to specific "boards" or other approval authorities. In these cases, the initial vocational and theoretical preparation is typically done in the university setting, accompanied by internships or residency requirements where experienced professionals ensure practical competencies as well as theoretical knowledge.

Everything we have talked about so far are merely entry level requirements, and a Level III professional is looking for something higher—perhaps even the *highest*—level of performance. That poses a serious challenge.

The problems with authority-defined standards

There are many organizations in the world that continually grapple with the challenge of keeping everyone "up to speed" with the standards employees once possessed at the time of their initial hiring and evaluation. This gave rise to something referred to as "currency based" training where recurrent training to industry defined (minimum) standards are conducted on a set schedule, typically annually or biannually. This type of spoon feeding creates the impression in many Level I or Level II professionals that if they really need to know something, it will be provided to them by the system. Obviously, if you are looking to grow, this is not a reasonable approach.

This "feed me" mindset was made clear to me recently when I read a critique from a 25-year professional in a high-risk industry.

> Handing out books with the courseware is a waste. If you expect anyone to do any outside reading, you better find a way to get us paid to do it.

Sad, but insightful.

Other industries, such as health care and education, rely on continuing education credits (CEUs) to keep their employees on step with compliance and new information. These are usually achieved through a variety of methods such as online courses, attendance at seminars, or videos, but regardless of the format, they are always approved by certified faculty or industry experts. We will look at this model more closely in our next chapter on *continuous improvement*.

The challenge of vocational excellence begins by questioning the current state of affairs.

In *Blue Threat* (Chapter 3, *Personal Alchemy: Turning Human Performance Lead into Gold*), we looked closely at the performance

VOCATIONAL EXCELLENCE 155

evolution ladder and demonstrated how you have to break out of the cultural norms and "zone of mediocrity" to achieve true Level III excellence. Here is a brief description from that discussion for those who have not had the opportunity to read it.

In summary, we see three distinct zones of performance, illustrated in the figure below. The first—and worst—is the *Personal and Organizational Failure Zone*. Here we tread perilously close to the edge of failure and fight daily battles for survival in our professional and personal lives. Life seems to be one near miss after another and it seems just a matter of time before the hammer drops.

One step up, we often find ourselves in the middle of the proverbial bell-shaped curve with masses of working drones like ourselves, good enough to get by but firmly stuck in the *Crushing Grip of Mediocrity*. Here we may feel safe and secure, but we coexist with some performance robbing and potentially dangerous bedfellows.

> "By practicing precision and seeking perfection, we are also improving our readiness for the day when the world turns mean and we need to be near perfect just to survive."

For the few who have figured it out, *Normalized Excellence* is the key to both professional improvement and personal fulfillment (Level III performance). This is the true high performance zone where we aim small, miss small, and flirt with occasional perfection. We are aware that by practicing precision and seeking perfection, we are also improving our readiness for the day when the world turns mean and we need to be near perfect just to survive.[1]

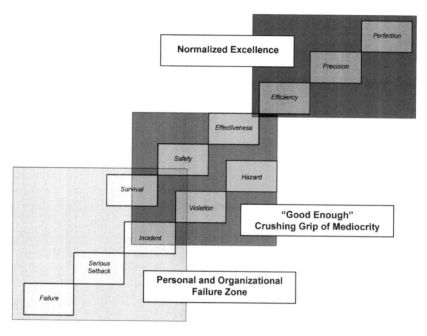

The Performance Evolution Ladder: Personal and Organizational Performance Zones

From this model, we see that recurrent training to minimum compliance standards is a professionalism trap that will hold us in the grip of Level I and Level II mediocrity unless we can find a means to grasp higher standards and pull ourselves out. The key to finding these handgrips is contained in our now familiar approach of a personal assessment followed by a set of specific tools to identify opportunities for improvement.

---

[1] Kern, Tony. *Blue Threat: Why to Err is Inhuman.* p. 56-57

Vocational excellence (job skills) (25%)

Try the following self-assessment to see where you perceive your professionalism with regards to *vocational excellence*. For each of the following questions, grade yourself by circling 0, .5, or 1 in accordance with the following criteria.

0	.5	1
Almost Never	**Sometimes**	**Nearly Always**

Vocational excellence is the next 25% of the professionalism equation. Let's see where we might still have some work to do.

I possess <u>mastery</u> levels of professional knowledge in all relevant areas, to include technical information, applicable regulations, organizational policies, and procedures.

0	.5	1

I am aware of what others are doing in my industry that set "above the bar" standards for industry best practices.

0	.5	1

I am capable of satisfactorily performing all the technical tasks for the job I've been trained for in both routine and non-routine situations.

0	.5	1

I have excellent interpersonal skills, and my coworkers know I function well in problem solving team projects.

0	.5	1

I maintain consistently high levels of situational awareness and exercise good judgment in both routine and non-routine situations.

0 .5 1

SUBTOTAL _____ x 5 = _____ (transfer this weighted score to the scorecard at the end of the book)

Keep one thing center in your mind as you think about your own talent level. High end professionals are <u>very</u> good at their primary jobs. It is critical to remember that *vocational excellence* involves both technical and nontechnical skills, and true experts master both. But no one masters the technical aspects of their job overnight, and the same is true for the nontechnical skills. Use the following roadblocks, ramps, and fast lanes to stay on track.

Technical credibility

Technical credibility is the knowledge and competency components of professionalism. Level III pros know their stuff, but also are aware that they will never know <u>everything</u> about their chosen vocation. Focus on the core ability to perform the technical aspects of the job you are trained for, and with continuous improvement, you will be recognized for your excellence by subordinates, peers, and supervisors.

Roadblocks

- Professional insecurity results in hiding weaknesses, stunting your professional growth.

VOCATIONAL EXCELLENCE 159

- Incapable of consistently performing all the tasks of the job but won't ask for guidance or instruction out of fear or embarrassment.
- Inability to accept legitimate criticism reduces constructive feedback from peers and supervisors, who learn to doubt your reliability.
- Failure to stay fully "up to speed" with new information or changes results in falling behind on new requirements and eventual poor performance.

On ramps

- Self check to ensure you are capable of satisfactorily performing all the tasks you've been trained for under normal and non-routine conditions. Be the first to identify a professional weakness.
- If you identify weak areas, assume others probably already know. Be humble and develop a personal improvement plan or ask for help.
- Everyone struggles with some aspect of their job, and the maturity to ask a mentor for some "over the shoulder" guidance is a sign of a true pro that can be counted on.

Fast lanes

- Master required and desirable knowledge of the technical information, principles, procedures, requirements, regulations, and policies related to your specialized expertise and how it relates to your organization's mission.
- Perform beyond what is expected for your level of experience. Be humble in excellence.

- Become the "go to" person in your organization on the tough tasks and hard-to-find information. Have your peers seek you out for assistance.

- Backstop your peers to ensure they are getting all the help they need, especially if it is something you can provide.

Technical credibility will take you far, but there will be times when you will be tempted or asked to go outside the lines of compliance. Level III pros expect these temptations and know how to handle them when they occur.

Personal discipline and compliance

A Level III pro understands and fully complies with all control systems and rules, including written and verbal authority. They understand where their decision space ends and who they need to ask for waiver authority if necessary. In the supervisory role, a Level III pro provides clear expectations and looks carefully for areas where deviance might be occurring. When noncompliant behavior is found, he or she deals with the problem first and then the person, but only if the person turns out to be the problem. Use these tools as a checklist to help accomplish this vital *vocational excellence* task.

Roadblocks

- Fails to fully learn or completely comprehend applicable guidance which results in noncompliance out of ignorance rather than intent.

- Justifies and excuses noncompliant actions in self and others because of "that's the way it's done around here" cultural norms.

- Follows the crowd into normalized deviance and noncompliance once the initial act of noncompliance occurs.
- "Mission hacker" attitude drives noncompliance to get things done outside the lines if that is what it takes.
- Shortcuts taken for convenience or when understaffed or fatigued.

On ramps

- Recognize and resist the temptation to deviate due to fatigue, staffing, or merely for convenience.
- Make sure you fully understand and can access all applicable guidance. When a question of compliance arises, look it up. If you can't find it, ask before you proceed under "assumed compliance."
- Practice the "3Ds" of Kevlar compliance—Attention to **d**etail, **d**iligence, and personal **d**iscipline.

Fast lanes

- Learn to master the BIG 4 to guide your actions: *Law, policy, shared values, conscience*—in that order. Share your rationale with others to build shared understanding of the BIG 4 framework for compliance.
- Correct and, if necessary, report noncompliant behaviors in the workplace in a tactful manner. Be able to explain the value of compliance to others with a risk-reward discussion.
- When in doubt, ask for clarification on vague verbal guidance, especially if you believe it conflicts with any written guidance

already in place. Then make sure to follow up to improve the vague guidance or communicate the organizational interpretation to others.

Level III personal discipline is built upon a detailed knowledge of all requirements and the confidence to challenge noncompliant norms.

Attention to detail

Level III pros accomplish all tasks with concern for all the areas involved, no matter how small. Some jobs need people who can handle both the small and large parts of a task, who won't overlook what needs to be done, and who can be depended on to do each task accurately and completely as a matter of routine excellence.

Roadblocks

- Doesn't finish well. Frequently fails to complete paperwork or hands off a task before it is completed.
- Accepts sloppy performance and incomplete work by coworkers and subordinates.
- Lowers standards and increases tolerance for errors and sloppiness when fatigued.

On ramps

- Avoid preoccupation or the "almost done" frame of mind. Stay on task until all items of a job are completed.
- Complete low-priority follow-up, including all electronic documentation and paperwork.

- Perform all routine and repetitive tasks with care and focused attention. Compare finished work against expectations.
- Recognize and correct distractions and mental drifting as they occur.

Fast lanes

- Think through the areas where you might be time constrained or task saturated, developing a plan for dealing with the challenges before they occur.
- Master the routine. Develop a keen eye for details in your own work as well as the work of others, especially in highly repetitive routine tasks.
- Finish strong. Spot incomplete work and encourage or assist others to drive every task to completion.
- Double check for errors and thoroughness when at the end of a task or assignment.

Some people are naturally good at details. I am not and have to make this aspect of vocational excellence a priority if I am to avoid the performance downgrade that comes with finishing poorly.

Diligence

Diligence is attention to detail over time. It means completing all the steps involved with a task to the best of your ability every time. It is a major differentiator between high achievers and the rest of the pack. When you get good at the little things, you get good at everything. Consider the following areas to improve your diligence.

Roadblocks

- Single, small acts of sloppiness "infect" your normally sound professionalism.
- Single deviations progress to frequent failures to follow through on details or low profile assignments.
- Time constraints, job pressures, or negative emotions toward your job, organization, supervisors, or team members erode diligence or attention to detail.

On ramps

- Follow Stephen Covey's advice by "beginning with the end in mind"[2] and picture your task as thoroughly completed to the highest standards before you even begin.
- Be predictably reliable by completing all tasks to standards as a matter of routine.
- Develop a persevering determination to perform tasks correctly and completely regardless of your emotional state.

Fast lanes

- Become "uncommonly reliable" through near perfect adherence to standards, timelines, and task requirements.
- Lead by <u>conspicuous example</u> when you observe others letting cultural norms, laziness, or sloppiness infect their performance.
- On complex tasks, develop a detailed integrated checklist (or use an existing one) to track all aspects of the project to completion.

---

[2] Stephen Covey. *7 Habits of Highly Effective People: Powerful Lessons for Personal Change.* Franklin Covey Company. 1990

VOCATIONAL EXCELLENCE 165

The preceding three areas, personal **d**iscipline, attention to **d**etail, and **d**iligence, have come to be known as the "3D" approach to world class compliance.[3] They are often overlooked in favor of more traditional nontechnical skills such as leadership and team training. Level III professionals will perform better in all of these traditional nontechnical factors precisely because they have mastered the 3Ds.

Nontechnical excellence

Nontechnical skills comprise a wide expanse of knowledge and abilities. This short list of key concepts will not get you to the expert level across the multiple areas in this vast landscape.

Although it cannot take the place of advanced nontechnical training programs offered by most organizations in areas such as leadership, followership, communications, team training, etc., it will provide some essential common reference points for beginning or continuing the journey towards Level III excellence.

Roadblocks

- Tendency to "go it alone" on complex tasks that should involve others leads to loss of effectiveness that might have been achieved with a team approach.

- Inability to control emotional reactions to ideas or actions from others you do not agree with shuts down communication channels.

---

[3] In Convergent Performance's proprietary *Global War on Error* programs, the "3D" approach is also known as "Kevlar Compliance" as an addition or complement to the "Swiss Cheese" system safety model. Their point is that there should be "no holes in compliance."

- Failure to accept appropriate leadership or followership role in a task or project degrades personal and/or team performance.
- Inability to function effectively in cross functional roles with personnel who are not a part of your daily work team.

On ramps

- Find and self-study resources on key nontechnical skills such as leadership communications and effective teamwork.
- Volunteer to attend any available formal training in nontechnical skills.
- Get comfortable working with others in leader, peer-to-peer, and follower roles, especially when you have an opportunity to participate in teams from areas you do not work with on a daily basis.
- In disagreements, focus on <u>what</u> is right, not <u>who</u> is right. Show maturity by being able to change your mind and position when the team wants to go in a direction you did not initially favor.

Fast lanes

- Stay focused on the task at hand when the team or coworkers wander. Gently guide discussion and team efforts back on task, even when you are not officially in a leadership role.
- Take time to learn the principles of some of the tougher nontechnical skills such as self-awareness, situation awareness (SA2), and cross functional team training.
- Seek opportunities to contribute to and optimize low profile or low performing teams. These are opportunities to polish your nontechnical game "off Broadway" while simultaneously building goodwill through voluntary contributions.

- Remain self-aware when emotions start to creep into your judgment and negatively impact your performance in any workplace setting.

As previously mentioned, entire books and university departments focus on single aspects of nontechnical excellence. Make learning these areas a focal area and the results will be swift and positive.

Now let's turn to the final area of vocational excellence, *problem solving*. Once again, there are many approaches to this critical skill, and only space to discuss the critical few that are key for achieving Level III professionalism.

> "Problem solving is considered to be among the most complex of our intellectual functions and currently the most difficult challenge for artificial intelligence (AI) advocates to solve enroute to their geek utopia of a computerized world."

Problem solving

American industrialist Henry Kaiser reportedly said that "problems are only opportunities in work clothes." Whenever we wish to move from a desired state to a new one, we have a problem that needs shaping and solving.

Problem solving is considered to be among the most complex of our intellectual functions[4] and currently the most difficult challenge for artificial intelligence (AI) advocates to solve enroute to their geek utopia of a computerized world. This is largely because problem

---

[4] Goldstein F. C., & Levin H. S. (1987). Disorders of reasoning and problem-solving ability. In M. Meier, A. Benton, & L. Diller (Eds.), *Neuropsychological rehabilitation*. London: Taylor & Francis Group.

solving involves multiple modes of thinking, including fact finding, problem framing, determination of what level of solution is needed, and resource discovery and allocation. In short, it's what humans do best, but Level III professionals do better than most. Consider the following tools and tips to get started or to keep improving your problem solving skills.

Roadblocks

- Inability to frame a problem and identify obstacles to success.
- Passive acceptance of fate when things begin to go wrong.
- Unwillingness to ask for assistance when you are unable to solve a problem on your own.

On ramps

- Identify and analyze problems in a timely manner appropriate for your level of experience and position.
- Learn to break complex problems into smaller ones and to find appropriate talent and resources to deconstruct the problem and construct the solution with efficiency.
- Have the courage to recommend solutions and offer insights and opinions when encountering problems in a team.
- Support the best solution offered by another when your solution is not accepted.

Fast lanes

- Learn about formal problem solving and investigation tools like *failure mode analysis, fault trees,* and *root cause analysis*. Pick one or more that might be relevant to your position (current or future) and master the technique.

- Weigh relevance and accuracy of information in individual and team problem solving.
- Test assumptions with probing questions like "what if this is not what we think it is?" This role is critical and can be filled even when you don't have great expertise in the area of concern.
- Learn to think laterally.[5] Generate alternative solutions to challenges to avoid "groupthink."

One of the fastest ways to the top of any field is to be an effective problem solver, but like all professionalism attributes, it takes dedicated attention to develop world class skills in this area. However, because it is key to rapid advancement, it might be worth some prioritization, especially for entry level and middle managers striving to get noticed.

Summary

As a young pilot in the United States Air Force, I was always measuring myself against the other aviators. The question of "who's the best pilot in the squadron?" was always on our minds, and as inexperienced, testosterone fueled jet jocks, we didn't really have a clue. So in the absence of what true professionalism was, we tried to out fly each other. Who flew the tightest formation, the best bomb drops, or the smoothest landings? While the friendly competition

---

[5] The term *lateral thinking* was coined by Edward de Bono in the book *New Think: The Use of Lateral Thinking* published in 1967. It is solving problems through an indirect and creative approach, using reasoning that is not immediately obvious and that may not be obtainable by using only traditional step-by-step logic or problem solving techniques.

certainly made us better at these small skill sets, it did little to prepare us as future professionals. The idea was that once we mastered the technical skill sets, we could move on to the "leadership stuff."

In retrospect, this was a serious mistake, and I think it remains so in many professions today. I don't know what the professional equivalent is for the tight formation for a young doctor, fire fighter, or bank manager, but most high achievers can work on more than technical skills early in their career. In point of fact, young men and women are actually much more capable of learning and integrating than those who have already established "hardening of the categories." It is time for a more holistic and integrated approach to vocational excellence and time to give young high achievers the full spectrum of opportunity. It is my hope that organizations will recognize the value of the Level III concept and make this a reality. In the meantime, the opportunity for highly motivated achievers to rapidly advance across the spectrum of professionalism on their own is now here.

Vocational excellence and professional ethics form fully half of the Level III professionalism equation. Now it is time to add the next 20% of the sum—*continuous improvement*.

VOCATIONAL EXCELLENCE **171**

"*In any profession, we must grapple with systems, resources, circumstances, people—and our own shortcomings as well. Yet somehow we must advance, we must refine, we must improve.*"

Atul Gwande, M.D.

Author of
Better: A Surgeon's Notes on Performance

Chapter 8

The Critical Importance of Continuous Improvement

"If you stop learning, you will forget what you already know."
Proverbs 19:27 (Contemporary English Version)

IMPORTANCE OF CONTINUOUS IMPROVEMENT

To stand still is to retreat.

The illusion of maintaining one's competency through repetition to minimum standards is only true in a static world—and we do not live in one of those. On a previous page, Dr. Atul Gwande points to the difficulties we face, but is dead on target when he uses the term *must* three times.

"We must advance. We must refine. We must improve."

But how?

In this chapter, we will look at the means of continuous improvement that go beyond the fundamentals of *deliberate practice* discussed in an earlier chapter. As in previous chapters, we will provide you the opportunity to assess your current status, as well as the *roadblocks, on ramps,* and *fast lane* tools to take immediate action in this vital domain of professionalism. First, let's begin with an issue we introduced briefly in *Blue Threat*, a simple but vital concept known to psychologists as *locus of control.*

Locus of control is how you view the cause and effect of what happens in your life. An internal locus of control says, "I am in charge of my destiny." Conversely, a total external locus says, "I am at the mercy of forces beyond my control."

Obviously, both internal and external factors play a role in the real world, but it is our perspective on *how much of a role each plays* that is critical to continuous improvement.

Many Level I and Level II professionals do not seek higher ground because they believe they are constrained by circumstances. But to become a Level III pro, we must take an internal locus of control—even when circumstances or resources *are* limiting our growth. Why? Because circumstances will *always* be somewhat limiting, and if we use the excuse that we cannot move forward until something changes, we will waste valuable time and miss multiple opportunities. We also are developing a mindset that rationalizes and favors the status quo. We will grow old, but not better.

> "Many Level I and Level II professionals do not seek higher ground because they believe they are constrained by circumstances."

One of my favorite quotes is from author Evangeline Wilkes and expresses the concern of waiting for circumstances to change.

"On the sands of hesitation, lay the bones of countless millions, who at the dawn of victory, sat down to wait, and waiting, died." For someone seeking the highest levels of professionalism, waiting is quicksand.

To address this challenge, I've simplified and paraphrased the mental approach we introduced in *Blue Threat* into two simple bullets.

Blue Threats are the strengths and weaknesses in <u>you</u> that influence your performance.

Red Threats are the <u>other</u> things—external situations, conditions, and people—that influence your performance.

A Red Threat mindset is an external locus of control point of view. It speaks like this:

- "I wasn't told."
- "I haven't been trained properly."
- "They didn't give me enough time."
- "I didn't have the right equipment or enough resources."
- "I'm not being given the opportunity."

Fundamental mindset: "It's <u>their</u> fault."

A Blue Threat mindset combined with the deliberate practice of professionalism takes a different point of view and is the key to unlocking Level III professionalism.

- "I'll find out myself."
- "I'll improve my own performance."
- "I'll use the time I have or find a way to make more."
- "I'll get the resources I need."
- "I'll create my own opportunities."

Fundamental mindset: "There are limiting factors but it's my responsibility to work through them."[1]

---

[1] Thanks to Andrew O'Connor for this simplified interpretation which is taken from the highly successful *Professional Journalist Cadet Training Program* at ABC Australia.

This simple change in personal philosophy opens the doors to a designable future filled with far more successes than if you choose a perspective that blames the world for your stagnation. Don't sit down to wait at the dawn of victory—press on in a planned manner that leverages the resources you have at your disposal.

Ad hoc vs. planned improvement

A Blue Threat/Going Pro mindset opens the door to daily, planned improvement, but we need more than an open door. We need a plan and tools to leverage the personal responsibility approach into continuous growth and ever higher levels of professionalism.

> "A Level II professional (fully compliant) who 'learns the ropes' through ad hoc experience can quickly fall victim to cultural norms of noncompliance in his day-to-day experience."

Plans are important, but the act of *planning* is perhaps moreso, especially when we juxtapose a solid continuous improvement plan against the alternative many of us have been taught to believe. You know it as the *experience is the best teacher* dogma that says we will naturally grow with time and experience. Here is the problem with that approach.

In many cases, experience teaches us the wrong lessons, and when this occurs, we actually get worse and not better. For example, a Level II professional (fully compliant) who "learns the ropes" through ad hoc experience can quickly fall victim to cultural norms of noncompliance in his day to day experience. This often occurs to new hires that come in with a great attitude and attention to detail, only to become jaded

IMPORTANCE OF CONTINUOUS IMPROVEMENT

and disillusioned by witnessing less-than-professional performance levels in their peers. The softer path of low performance beckons and peer pressure seals the door behind them. Learning from experience, they quickly fall down the ladder of professionalism. Worse through experience, not better.

The following figure illustrates an unplanned, ad hoc professional journey based solely on experience.

> "The softer path of low performance beckons and peer pressure seals the door behind them. Learning from experience, they quickly fall down the ladder of professionalism. Worse through experience, not better."

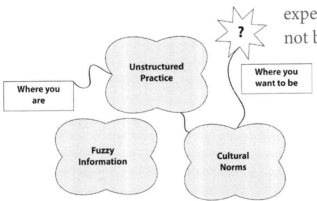

Unplanned, "experience is the best teacher" approach

Of course, experience *can* be a wonderful teacher, when accompanied by planning and tools to mine relevant lessons for improvement from your daily experiences. Planned improvement leverages experience but measures against known professionalism standards, provides metrics for improvement, and involves the known path of deliberate practice. It looks more like this next figure.

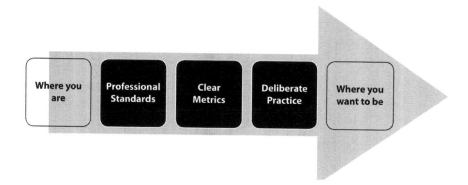

Planned improvement based on structured experience, feedback, and deliberate practice

The planned approach is a direct path to your goals. It does require some up front work and personal discipline, but the end state is certainly more predictable and worth the effort.

Case study: Here I come, ready or not.

Let's see how this planned approach to professionalism plays in the real world. The following letter was sent to me by a friend and colleague who is a television journalist in Australia[2] and who has been using the personal improvement approach for several years. I believe it hits the key dangers of an ad hoc improvement approach, as well as the value of a toolkit to employ under extreme conditions.

> I still remember sitting there in the crowd as you put up the slide[3] showing the ladder of precision, and highlighted the "crushing grip

---

[2] Hence the British spelling in the letter

[3] Working with the Australian Civil Aviation Safety Authority (CASA), I had conducted a series of professionalism workshops across Oz in the summer of 2009. This gentleman attended my presentation in Perth.

of mediocrity." It was at that point that I realised that's exactly where I was, and had been, for some years. After leaving my previous company, I'd made a conscious decision to place family first, and work second. It was the right and proper thing to do with three young children.

But what I underestimated was the insidious nature of mediocrity. By hitting cruise control on my career, I also started to lower the bar. I did a job that I could do competently on two cylinders. I was rarely pushed or challenged. I became a spectator as radical changes swept through our organisation, demanding new skills and capabilities from our on-the-road reporters.

I was competent, comfortable, and complacent. And I was blind to the fact that I was being left behind, quietly being de-skilled as the bar was raised, and the escalator silently shuttled me downwards.

We will come back to the rest of the letter in a few paragraphs and see how the structured approach to professional growth can be applied, even under extreme conditions, to turn the tide from complacency towards continuous improvement.

But before we do, let's provide a bit of structure on how to create the plan itself.

"Gimme three steps"

There is a hard rocking Lynyrd Skynyrd ballad from the 1970s titled *Gimme Three Steps* that tells the tale of a young man who gets caught unawares in a dangerous position. While dancing with "a girl named Linda Lou," ... "in walked a man with a gun in his hand, lookin' for you know who." The songwriter's plea to his would-be assassin to "gimme three steps" was in essence a desperate request for a head start, and a bit of room to maneuver to outrace a situation he did not see coming that had turned ugly fast.

Maybe my rock n' roll metaphor is a bit of a stretch, but if you had to make a sudden break from the dangerous grip of mediocrity that had stunted your professional growth; if you needed some room to maneuver, where would you go? Try these three steps for planned improvement to see if they might work in your world.

Step 1. Innovate. Lots of people misunderstand innovation. They think it requires great creativity or some form of new age brainstorming technique. In truth, *innovation* is nothing so mystical. The word comes from the Latin noun *innovatus* which literally translates as "into the new." In some cases, innovation is a personal choice to improve on a predetermined schedule; in others, the requirement is thrust upon them unannounced like a pop quiz of our professional readiness. Such was the case with our intrepid Australian reporter who was forced "into the new" to meet an unforeseen challenge.

> *The first shock came when my boss decided to put me back on the road as a reporter. I'd last been a reporter in 1994, but since then had been in supervisory roles. Steven Pressfield quotes Telemon of Arcadia as saying "It is one thing to study war. It is another to live the warrior's life." Managerial roles can shield you from the real work and in times of great change, you can forget how much you've forgotten, and lose your appreciation of the difference between doing the work, and telling others how to do it.*
>
> *I set myself a program of professional development based on "Blue Threat" and made reasonable progress with the routine demands of domestic reporting. But my day of reckoning was coming. It arrived*

on the 15th of December 2010 when a boat carrying 92 people was shipwrecked on Christmas Island in the Indian Ocean. Fifty people died as the boat was smashed on the rocky cliffs in heavy seas. Normally, a foreign correspondent would be dispatched to the scene of such a major story.

Through a combination of personnel and logistical limitations, it fell to the Perth office of the ABC to send a reporter. I was the most senior reporter, yet oddly the one with the least amount of recent reporting experience. As I packed my bags, I thought of your line in "Redefining Airmanship" about proficiency. "Confidence is only justified if you've done it recently and done it well." I qualified on neither account.

This gentleman was fortunate in that when the pop quiz came, he had already been working on something he could turn to. He had an innovative option at hand.

The Latin proverb *fortes fortuna adiuvat*—or *fortune favors the bold*—is the motto of the 366th Fighter Wing at Mountain Home Air Force Base in Idaho. When it comes to Level III professionalism, fortune favors the bold innovator.

Step 2. Integrate. Innovations are not solutions. They are purely theoretical constructs until put into action. We all know "idea men" who can't make new ideas work in the real world. The vital connection between innovation and your desired end state is *integration into your daily activities*. In many ways, this step is more difficult than any other as innovation involves changing modes of thought, whereas integration involves changing modes of action. Both involve courage and demand follow through to make the desired change stick.

To make this integration task easier, I have ensured that each professionalism domain chapter in this book provides a toolkit in the form of the *roadblocks, on ramps,* and *fast lanes*. If you are even contemplating the Going Pro approach, take the tough step now and integrate these applied skills into your daily activities. One easy way to remember the link between innovation and integration is with the simple phrase *into the new in all that I do*.

Let's see how the pop professionalism quiz is going for our journalism colleague as he attempts to integrate new applied skills in an extreme and demanding environment.

> We got to the airport. The camera operator got offloaded because of seat unavailability. I landed on the island and had to battle through providing coverage for radio, television, and online for two days before another crew could arrive. I had no confidence, only the conviction that I needed to find a way to get the job done. Throughout I used "Blue Threat" to keep me focused on doing the work and simultaneously working the problems. Time and again these words and concepts would come back to me as I struggled to get back up to speed under the pressure of filing stories up to 20 times a day.

The key here is not that everything worked, but rather that in an extreme environment with low proficiency; he had a set of tools available. As you read this encounter, you get the sense of someone who knows they are being tested and is enjoying the moment. Far from being in over his head, this gentlemen seems to understand this is a "learn as you go" event and is actually tinkering with his professionalism approach as he confronts the onslaught of challenges. The insight of using new *professionalism* tools (as opposed to technical journalistic tools) for "doing the work and simultaneously working the problems . . . as I struggled to get back up to speed" is a powerful testimony of how nontechnical skills are often the most critical in some settings.

IMPORTANCE OF CONTINUOUS IMPROVEMENT 185

There is one more critical step to drive the improvement from an applied tool into a continuous learning <u>process</u>.

Step 3. Calibrate. The final step is using specific standards to measure and refine performance—*calibration*. Unless you have a degree is psychometrics and statistics, this requires a little help.

Calibration against defined professionalism standards is a form of *kaizen*, a Japanese term for the routine process of continuous improvement. In *Blue Threat*, we explained the use of the *Blue Threat Report and Analysis Tool* (BRAT) to quantify the numbers, nature, and specific types of errors one commits. Over time, this leads to the development of personal error pattern (PEP) recognition and personal operating procedures (POP) against key areas. If BRATs, PEPs, and POPs aren't ringing any bells, pick up a copy of *Blue Threat* and review Chapter 6, *Proof of Life: Error Control in Action*.

The Going Pro program also provides solid measuring sticks in the forms of professionally developed assessments (see appendix), but also through the regular use of the multiple professional inventories at the end of these chapters. This is the 21st century and I realize that text based solutions are SO old school, so in short order there will be "an app for that" that provides daily reminders and tools for the routine and deliberate tracking of professionalism skills.

Speaking of calibration in the real life workplace, let's return to the Indian Ocean to see how the integration of professionalism skills played out.

> *It was a brutal lesson where I felt the pain of allowing myself to be trapped in the crushing grip of mediocrity. Despite my lack of proficiency, the trip was successful. The network has since sent me*

back three times to cover detention centre riots, boat arrivals, and other immigration issues. I've used the Blue Threat approach to do <u>after assignment reviews to identify the fail points and the fixes.</u>

It's been vital in not only equipping me to deal with the demands of remote reporting, <u>it's helped formulate a standard organisational approach to covering the island, and provided a framework for training and supporting other reporters.</u> (emphasis added)

Nice job, eh? Note the underlined items, where the error control metrics were used not only to persevere against the multiple challenges he faced, but also to analyze and share the data he had gathered to improve the overall capacity of the organization and support his peers. Although I am jumping ahead to our next chapter, this describes Level III *professional engagement* nearly perfectly. He continues to use the tools that worked so well in his new position, a clear indication that he is back on the professional fast track.

Now, let's see where you perceive your current position with regards to *continuous improvement*.

Continuous Improvement (20%)

For each of the following questions, grade yourself by circling 0, .5, or 1 in accordance with the following criteria.

0	.5	1
Almost Never	**Sometimes**	**Nearly Always**

I routinely pursue higher levels of professional knowledge on my own time.

0	.5	1

IMPORTANCE OF CONTINUOUS IMPROVEMENT 187

I debrief or conduct after action reviews on all operational activities for lessons learned, and gratefully accept peer criticism.

      0   .5   1

I am getting noticeably better with experience.

      0   .5   1

I refine my performance against personal benchmarks that exceed industry standards.

      0   .5   1

I assume new responsibilities at each opportunity to do so.

      0   .5   1

SUBTOTAL _____ x 4 = _____ (transfer this weighted score to the scorecard at the end of the book)

If you are not improving, odds are you are getting worse at what you do, even with greater experience. Careers are made or lost on the fulcrum of voluntary improvement. Ask yourself, *what can I become, by virtue of what I do here and now with my time and efforts and the resources at hand?* Then use the concepts below to drive higher levels of professional performance.

> "Ask yourself, what can I become, by virtue of what I do here and now with my time and efforts and the resources at hand?"

Let's begin by looking at our current perception of *excellence*.

Vision of excellence

It's difficult to improve if you don't have a clear picture of where you want to go. This skill involves being able to create or accept a mental model of performance at levels well above minimum standards.

Remove a few roadblocks and see what tools are available that fit your environment and situation.

Roadblocks

- Unaware of what the organizational vision is.
- Content with the status quo even if it is less than optimal.
- Goes with the flow and accepts cultural norms as the guiding standards of performance.
- "Good enough" mindset results in sliding standards of performance, stunting professional growth.

On ramps

- Ensure your personal vision of excellence aligns with and, ideally, exceeds the organizational vision.
- Use all available time and resources to optimize outcomes to highest standards possible within those constraints, even after you have met the minimum standards.
- Recognize areas where organizational and systemic improvement is possible with existing resources.

Fast lanes

- "Picture perfect" in order to establish new standards for improvement.

- Take a long-term view and build a shared vision of excellence with coworkers that exceeds that mandated by others.
- Act as a catalyst for change by influencing coworkers to translate a vision of excellence into actions that create new cultural norms.

A senior Vice President of Quality Improvement at a large defense contractor once told me that the hardest thing he had to do was getting people to "define higher standards in the absence of externally defined mandates."

Differentiating performance

Breaking out of cultural norms is nearly impossible without being able to differentiate performance levels above the line of "acceptable performance." This skill involves being able to make fair and sound assessments of performance in yourself and others, without being biased by internal or external factors. If you are struggling in this regard, see if there are any tools available here to drive this new competency.

Roadblocks

- Unable or unwilling to discriminate performance levels in self or others beyond outcome-only criteria ("It worked, so what's the problem?").
- Unable or unwilling to discriminate performance beyond cultural norms ("That's the way we've always done it here").
- Biased evaluation based on personal likes and dislikes of individuals, not performance.

On ramps

- Cultivate the ability to recognize and assess performance against all established standards.
- Train yourself to look for differences in performance levels, not merely task accomplishment.
- Make fair and unbiased assessments based upon measures that include observable behaviors, performance feedback, and demonstrated results.

Fast lanes

- Cultivate the ability to recognize and assess performance at discrete levels above and below established standards in multiple areas such as situational awareness, teamwork, and the amount of learning that took place during the task.
- Fight for negative feedback to avoid confirmation bias.
- Be able to discern differences with connoisseurship through the use of advanced training, observation tools, and techniques. (see appendix for specific tools currently available.)
- The ability to recognize discrete performance across multiple areas is the mark of a Level III pro. It also leads to *continual learning*, our next topic of discussion.

Continual learning

An instructor pilot once told me that no matter how many flying hours I accrued, a professional pilot never forgets that they are always a student in an airplane, and the world was a cruel teacher that gave quizzes wherever and whenever it wanted. The price of failing the quiz was often a funeral and a widow who would probably remarry some other guy in the squadron. He got my attention.

This skill requires internally established learning goals and growth-based development of knowledge skills and abilities that meet or exceed job expectations.

Roadblocks

- Attends only required training, but with lack of enthusiasm or genuine improvement agenda.
- "Bad mouths" organizational learning programs or instructors.
- Comfortable with the status quo.

On ramps

- Always carry a small notebook and pen or pencil. Life gives us dozens of improvement lessons every day if we are ready to capture them.
- Develop a personal learning plan based on accurate self-assessed strengths and weaknesses.
- Take advantage of formal self-development programs when the opportunities arise.

Fast lanes

- Find a mentor. It doesn't have to be Yoda, but make it someone you can learn the right lessons from.
- Be a mentor. You learn most and best what you teach.
- Take the initiative to continuously advance knowledge and performance through self-defined means inside and outside of the work environment.

- Get off the recurrent training cycle by embracing "growth-based" development of knowledge skills and abilities that exceed job expectations.

Make learning fun by making the time to dig into things you enjoy learning about. But don't forget the weak areas, which require an accurate self-assessment of your current state.

Objective self-assessment

Improvement begins with dissatisfaction with the status quo, which in turn requires each of us to be able to accurately see where we can, and need, to improve. If we can learn to be a bit harder on ourselves and provide the requisite negative feedback from less than optimum performance, objective self-assessment can truly drive the improvement effort almost by itself.

Roadblocks

- Rationalizes or externalizes reasons for errors and missed opportunities.
- No habit or process for objective self-assessment.
- Personal view of strengths and weaknesses differ significantly from coworkers' and supervisors' assessments of your performance.

On ramps

- Begin conducting self-debriefs and after-action evaluations of personal performance.
- Seek peer and supervisor input to align accuracy of self-assessments.

- Recognize personal errors and missed opportunities and take specific steps to avoid repeats.

Fast lanes

- Use a formal tool or system to recognize and track personal errors and missed opportunities (see BRAT in *Blue Threat*). Data-driven improvements tend to stick.

- Identify and trend personal performance over prolonged periods to objectively identify what is working and what isn't.

- Tailor continuous improvement efforts towards known and written personal improvement goals.

To "know thyself is the font of all wisdom," but you also have to be able to bounce back from adversity, which leads us to our final sub-domain of *continuous improvement*.

Resiliency

In the aftermath of a mistake, compromise, or setback, *resiliency* is the capacity to "bounce back" to a previous state of normal functioning, or using the experience of exposure to adversity to produce a "steeling effect" and function better than expected.

High achievers are often very hard on themselves. While this can be a good thing for *objective self-assessment*, it can result in short term distraction and even longer bouts of depression. Make sure you have an accurate self-image, but then give yourself a break when the inevitable mistakes do come.

Roadblocks

- Suffers from "emotional jetlag" where incessant worry about consequences of a previous mistake or outcome erodes confidence and focus.
- "Scapegoating" thoughts and activities to assign blame to others rather than learning from adversity.
- Doesn't deal effectively with pressure; pessimism grows adversity.

On ramps

- After a mistake or poor outcome, consciously commit to bounce back to normal functioning rapidly.
- Deal effectively with pressure; remain optimistic and persistent, even when things aren't going well.
- Pick up a teammate who has just made a mistake. The favor will likely be returned in the future.

Fast lanes

- Learn to "take a hit" gracefully. Use setbacks to motivate higher performance by bouncing back with greater strength and concentration.
- Use bouts with adversity to produce a "steeling effect" and function with greater confidence under future adverse conditions.

Resiliency teaches the ability to cope with stress, and even to thrive in high-stress situations. As the final element of *continuous improvement*, the ability to recover quickly and learn the right lessons from setbacks completes our picture of this third domain of professionalism.

Summary

We have discussed multiple aspects of this vital piece of the professionalism puzzle, but it is appropriate that we conclude with the final installment of the letter from our stalwart journalist to see what the endgame was with his bout with adversity and journey back to excellence.

> *As for me, I'm about to start a new role as a current affairs presenter on our Perth-based program "730WA." It's a new challenge hosting a program and conducting studio interviews. After my day of reckoning, I feel like I'm catching up and grinding out clicks on the micrometre of progress.*

This last sentence is a classic kaizen approach to professionalism. While kaizen usually delivers small improvements, the culture of continual, aligned small improvements and the organizational standardization that <u>learns</u> from innovative individuals yields large results through compound improvement. In short, professionalism improvements that start with a single individual can dramatically impact an entire culture. We will discuss this "ripple up" phenomenon further in a later chapter on culture.

But before we do, we have a few more domains of Level III professionalism to dissect, and while they are weighted slightly lower than the previous domains, they are just as important to creating the full Level III package. The next stop is *professional engagement*.

"Try everything. Join everything. Meet everybody."

Hedy Lamarr, Actress

Chapter 9

Professional Engagement: Where the Rubber Meets the Road

"The more you engage with customers, the clearer things become and the easier it is to determine what you should be doing."

John Russell, Senior Executive, Harley Davidson

PROFESSIONAL ENGAGEMENT

"No man is an island." The words of English poet John Donne were true when he wrote them in the 16th century and remain sound guidance for those who would seek Level III professionalism nearly six centuries later. Twenty-first century business and government is intrinsically linked, and the ability to engage with formal and informal touch points in the public, organization, and industry at large are key elements of a Level III professional's toolkit.

> *"Professional engagement* goes well beyond communications or so-called 'people skills' and focuses upon a professional's ability to confidently interact with the entire system around them."

Professional engagement goes well beyond communications or so-called "people skills" and focuses upon a professional's ability to confidently interact with the entire system around them. Like all aspects of the new professionalism, it is a planned approach based upon specific competencies. It is important to be in a constant state of readiness to deploy these new competencies as some of the most challenging interactions will be thrust upon us without notice. Most others will come on schedule. A few we must find and reach out to.

Professional engagement is the domain of professionalism that brings our Level III skills out of the isolation of "personal improvement" and puts them into play in the real world. It is where the rubber meets the road.

Many points of contact are mandated by our occupational roles. For example, a sales associate has little choice in whether or not they interact with their clients (at least not for long if they don't), but an IT programmer may not have the same level of mandated interactions. Many of our interactions can be planned and carefully choreographed, others are chance encounters. Some interactions are completely positive, others combative. In a global economy, there are language and cultural concerns, generational, gender, and personality differences. Working well with this mix of people is challenging, to say the least.

Add to these challenges the societal and workplace trends that tend to isolate individuals behind cubicle walls, virtual offices, or *Facebook* pages. Our uncertain economic future has many professionals changing employers, and even occupations, multiple times during their career. Put it all together, and you have an environment that provides the opportunity for professional growth and further separation from the pack. In the modern workplace, *professional engagement* has never been more important.

Through it all, the words of the English poet echo across the centuries.

> *No man is an island entire of itself; every man is a piece of the continent, a part of the main;... any man's death diminishes me, because I am involved in mankind. And therefore never send to know for whom the bell tolls; it tolls for thee.*[1]

If we don't take Donne's reference to death literally, we see the link. Anyone's *failure, loss of passion,* or *unprofessional act* ripples throughout the system, subtly impacting and diminishing the whole at some level.

To put it in less poetic terms—we are all in this damn thing together.

Modern professionals must understand and manage this evolving interconnectedness and do so elegantly and fluidly in a constantly changing business and regulatory environment. This is what *professional engagement* is all about.

In this chapter, we will speak to this challenge from four perspectives. We will look at engagement between:

A professional and their customer

A professional and their coworkers

A professional and their organization

A professional and their industry

In each case, we will look at how these interactions impact the development of the professional through mutually beneficial relationships. We will also see that each of these relationships, although different, relies on a strikingly similar set of professionalism competencies.

---

[1] John Donne (1572-1631) "No Man is an Island" (partial quotation)

Let's jump start this discussion with a topic that has become almost an oxymoron in some industries and organizations—*customer service*.

Customer service—a lost art?

No matter what job you have, you have *customers*. As the CEO of a small business, I have the paying customers our company serves, as well as the employees that I serve, and the Partners of the company that oversee our operations. Likewise, a government official's customers are the public, as well as the interagency customers that rely on them to do their jobs as a part of the public service whole. An airline maintenance technician's customers might include the pilots, other airfield contractors, etc. A church pastor's customers are her congregation, as well as the rest of the church staff. A husband's customers are his wife and children, as well as his work-related customer list.

"You only get one chance to make a first impression."

We all have customers, so we all have a need for customer service as a core professionalism skill.

In chapter 1, we pointed out how the information age has changed the impact a single act of poor customer service can have. Engagement between people leaves lasting impressions. This is true regardless of the communication medium that is used. A short, unprofessional email or text message can be as damaging as a face-to-face altercation. In fact, it can often be more damaging, as electronic transmissions leave a permanent—and forwardable—trail.

There are entire courses and companies dedicated to this topic, and it is not my intent to try and duplicate their depth of expertise here. What we can do is share a few central themes that can help us build up this important aspect and grow our professionalism.

- **Make a good first impression.** You only get one chance to make a first impression with a customer you are engaging with for the first time. People remember and value initial contacts. I once worked for an Air Force Brigadier General named Phil Ford, who told us, "there are only two places anyone enters this base, the Front Gate and Base Operations at the airfield. Put your best people there and remind them every day they are our ambassadors."

  First impressions are also important with people you work with every day, your <u>internal</u> customers. We will discuss this more in a follow on section on coworker interaction, but if you treat <u>everyone</u> as a customer, you get not only their respect and cooperation, but also a heck of a lot more practice.

- **Establish a human connection first.** People approach each other with their guard up because they don't know what to expect from you. First names are a great place to start, beginning with your own. Something as simple as answering the phone with "Hello, this is John," can humanize the discussion from the start. You have to exercise some caution here as

> "One of the core beliefs of Level III professionals is that there are no insignificant people, and there are no insignificant problems."

there are also issues of titles and protocol that can get in the way. Be careful to know and use the correct titles (Doctor, Professor, General, etc.) until they clear you to do otherwise.

The next step is to make a connection with something as trivial, such as "Thanks for calling, it's a great day here in Colorado, what's the weather like where are you calling from?" Electronic communication is no different, but obviously needs to be tailored a bit. The main point is to let them know you are going to be easy to work with. Don't overdo this, as it can lead to problems with the next key to customer service.

> "Authentic respect is easy to recognize and is often rewarded."

- **Respect their time.** Everyone is busy, so after establishing the person-to-person connection, get down to business. Whether they are a paying customer, an internal customer, or just someone who stops by your office because they can't find their way to a local address, strive for efficient communications that addresses their need and respects their schedule.

- **Respect their perspective and position.** One of the core beliefs of Level III professionals is that there are no insignificant people, and there are no insignificant problems. Regardless if you are talking to the CEO of a mega-corporation or an intern with a question, take them and their problem seriously. Don't fake it, mean it. I have heard of dozens of cases where someone who came to a person or company for something trivial and was impressed with the way they were treated came back with business, sometimes big business. Authentic respect is easy to recognize and is often rewarded.

PROFESSIONAL ENGAGEMENT 205

- **Show some urgency.** Not every problem is an emergency and not every customer will come to you with a crisis that needs solving. But everyone appreciates someone who will put in the extra effort to assist them in whatever their issue might be. In today's economy, speed is a competitive advantage. If you let a customer (internal or external) know that you are someone who will "get off the dime" to assist them with their challenge, your reputation for great customer service will grow, along with your professionalism.

    Even if you are not the one who can help them, don't just "pass the buck." Introduce them to the appropriate person or resource and let them know they can always come back to you if they have another issue. Note that the "appropriate person or resource" may not even be inside your company or organization. Nothing builds credibility like recommending another person or company when you do not have the resources or expertise to meet the customer's need.

- **Find common ground.** Some people still think this is solely a sales technique, but if used properly, you can build long term bridges to world-class customer service. As you are actively listening to your customer, look for things you have in common. It might be golf, traveling, or a favorite band. Be careful that this common ground is something positive, as there are dangerous pitfalls

> "In today's economy, speed is a competitive advantage. If you let a customer (internal or external) know that you are someone who will 'get off the dime' to assist them with their challenge, your reputation for great customer service will grow, along with your professionalism."

out there, such as religion, politics, or common frustrations with others in your industry. Keep it above board, and establish a connection that will last beyond the current issue.

- **Make a good final impression.** There is a rule of thumb among professional speakers that if you start strong and finish strong, you can get away with a few things that are less-than-perfect in the middle. The same is true with customer service. Commit to follow through or follow up; then make sure you do. A phone call or email the day after the initial contact will reassure your customer that you are responsive. Staying positive can be a tough challenge at the end of a long day, when both you and your customer may be fatigued and frustrated. This is when the real pros show their stuff by staying helpful. Remember to thank them for reaching out to you. End every customer interaction on a good note.

- **Above all, be friendly.** No matter how good a professional you are, you can't solve every problem for every customer. People will overlook a lot if they are convinced you are someone they can work with and enjoy interacting with.

> "If you start strong and finish strong, you can get away with a few things that are less-than-perfect in the middle."

Customer service is a core competency for every professional, and Level III professionals will excel here. Many of these same skills apply to another challenge in the modern workplace: coworker interaction.

Engaging with coworkers: More than a matter of civility

Coworkers are internal customers, but ones we work with on a regular and continuing basis. Coworkers include superiors, subordinates, and peers who may be employees of the company, or in many cases "permanent contractors" who support a particular company or organization. No matter how talented one is, coworkers can make or break a professional's effectiveness. According to researchers at the American Psychological Association, things are not so good between coworkers in the modern workplace.

> "People will overlook a lot if they are convinced you are someone they can work with and enjoy interacting with."

Workplace incivility" is on the rise, researchers said Sunday at the American Psychological Association annual meeting in August 2011. The academics define workplace incivility as "a form of organizational deviance ... characterized by low-intensity behaviors that violate respectful workplace norms, appearing vague as to intent to harm."[2]

Intent to harm? That is a <u>long</u> ways from treating coworkers as internal customers with Level III customer service skills. "When we look at the actual behaviors that are considered a part of workplace incivility, we see rudeness, insults, disrespect, and

> "No matter how talented one is, coworkers can make or break a professional's effectiveness."

---

[2] *USA Today*, online edition found at http://yourlife.usatoday.com/parenting-family/story/2011/08/Incivility-a-growing-problem-at-work-psychologists-say/49854130/1

bad manners on the list. It's a growing and prevalent problem," said Jeannie Trudel of Indiana Wesleyan University-Marion, the author of one study on the topic.

So what is behind this apparent problem? Experts blame the economy, which seems to have become the hobgoblin for every business challenge we face.

> As companies buy out and lay off workers while expecting to keep productivity up, the niceties suffer, suggests psychologist and researcher Paul Fairlie of Toronto: "White-collar work is becoming a little more blue-collar. There's higher work demands, longer hours. When you control for inflation, people are getting paid less than in the late '60s. A lot of people are working much harder. They've got fluid job descriptions and less role clarity. So for some people, for a growing fringe, work is becoming more toxic."[3]

The term "growing fringe" is more than a little spooky, and it should be. Workplace violence is the natural outgrowth of incivility, and it is also on the upswing. According to the U.S. Department of Labor's Bureau of Labor Statistics published fact sheet, workplace shootings account for roughly 10% of all work-related deaths per annum in the United States. While this number may seem shockingly high, it is accurate and getting worse:

---

[3] *USA Today*, online edition found at http://yourlife.usatoday.com/parenting-family/story/2011/08/Incivility-a-growing-problem-at-work-psychologists-say/49854130/1

Over the past 5 years, 2004-08, an average of 564 work-related homicides occurred each year in the United States. In 2008, a total of 526 workplace homicides occurred, or 10% of all fatal work injuries.[4]

Workplace violence resulting in death is now the second highest cause of work-related deaths in America, trailing only behind transportation fatalities of workers killed in highway accidents.[5]

Not to make light of this tragic situation, but killing your coworker has to rank pretty high on the list of unprofessional acts.

So what is the point here?

The place you work in every day, and the people you work with every day, may represent your best opportunity and point of greatest impact for your professional engagement skills. Recall from our discussion of deliberate practice in chapter 5 that three primary components of the technique were required to make it work:

- The practice of the tasks could be repeated a lot
- Feedback was continuously available
- Mental demands were significant during practice sessions

From what we learned about the organizational climate in most modern workplaces, it appears we may be in the perfect setting to hone our professional engagement skill set through deliberate practice.

A modern professional must understand the factors that are behind the problem and recognize the professional engagement behaviors (positive and negative) and opportunities in oneself and coworkers.

---

[4] U.S. Dept. of Labor: Bureau of Labor Statistics, Workplace Violence Fact Sheet, July 2010

[5] U.S. Dept. of Labor: Bureau of Labor Statistics

In addition to the core customer service skills listed in the previous section, consider the following ideas for creating and sustaining positive interactions.

- **Hard on the problem, easy on the person.** Keep focusing on the problem as the problem and the people as the solution. Occasionally, the two will be tightly connected, but focusing attention on a person problem in the middle of a task often makes the situation worsen. Save the people issues for the after action reviews, or if it's too bad to endure, move your observations through the appropriate supervisory chain and human resources channels.

- **Think "around the corner" to a positive end state.** As you work the problems, think about how you create a positive experience from a tough challenge. For example, if you are at the end of a long workday or task, focus the discussion and your attitude on how good it will be to finish strong and look back with satisfaction on a job well done vs. the regret or frustration you will feel if you let things unravel over the last ten yards of the day or project.

- **Assume everyone is watching and listening.** In the modern workplace, there are very few well-kept secrets. Guard and guide your words and body language. Fight to stay optimistic and positive. There is an emotional tone to every human interaction and people are naturally attracted to those who stay strong and positive in the storms.

- **Take humor seriously.** The old adage that "laughter is the best medicine" is quite literally true in many cases. Everyone knows that one of the best stress reduction techniques known to modern science is laughter. Develop a sense of humor and don't be afraid to laugh out loud at the situation or yourself. Be careful about laughing at colleagues or their situations, unless you are certain they can take it—and give it back.

- **Reach out, across, up, and down.** Here are four words that will build more positive feelings and *esprit d'corps* than any others: "How can I help?" It might be something as simple as making copies for someone who is rapidly approaching a tough deadline, or offering to lend your truck and back to a colleague who is moving into a new apartment. People respond to those who recognize and assist them in times of need.

> "All organizations have requirements, but they also have desirements— things they can't mandate but that they hope you will do voluntarily."

Also find and be a mentor. Nothing advances professional competency like one-on-one mentorship. We will talk more about this in our upcoming chapter on *selflessness*.

Professional engagement with coworkers can and should be the most fulfilling piece of your professional growth program. When viewed from this perspective, it's really not a matter of *civility*—it's pure professionalism.

Engaging within the organization. All organizations have requirements, but they also have *desirements*—things they can't mandate but that they hope you will do voluntarily. These are things like participating in reporting systems, making suggestions, raising your hand for a volunteer project, or even signing up for the company volleyball team.

Of course, the <u>most</u> important piece of your relationship with your company or organization is to be technically competent and reliable. We covered that pretty well in our chapter on *vocational excellence*. So in addition to the tips and tools offered in the *roadblocks, on ramps,* and *fast lanes* at the end of the chapter, here are a few ideas to improve this area.

- **Look for existing engagement systems and opportunities.** Depending on who you work with or for, this might be easy or hard. Some organizations communicate their programs quite well, others barely at all. Simple steps like participating in safety and quality reporting systems are only simple if you know where to find the access points and build in the time and effort to use them. Make the effort to systematically identify the human and electronic points of contact for existing program elements such as safety, quality, organizational development, and morale and recreation programs, and then engage when and where appropriate. One more point, don't let cultural norms shape your participation just because a program is not popular or its sponsor is not someone you know or like.

  > "With a little courage and a few hours of work, she not only improved the entire organization, but jumped a few notches up the ladder of professional competence in the eyes of everyone in the company."

- **Cheerfully participate and encourage others to do so.** Obviously, time and workload constraints will partially dictate your level of participation in any non-mandatory systems or programs. But if you can make the mental adjustment to view these programs as a part of your job and build it in as such, you can turn what was once a burdensome addition into a positive professional growth opportunity.

- **Identify missing pieces and suggest or build them.** A few months ago, a new employee in our company came to me shortly after being hired and asked if we had a list of employee benefits. I responded off hand that all of those items "were in the employee handbook," unintentionally inferring that she hadn't yet looked for them there. As it turned out, there were many omissions in the handbook and those that were in there were difficult to find. A few days later, she and our office manager had voluntarily created a one-page synopsis of the entire benefits package and provided it to all employees. After eating a large slice of humble pie, I apologized for the oversight and thanked them both for their effort. With a little courage and a few hours of work, she not only improved the entire organization, but jumped a few notches up the ladder of professional competence in the eyes of everyone in the company.

The relationship between a professional and their organization is symbiotic and should be mutually beneficial. Many parts of the organizational support system often languish due to a wide variety of factors. With a little focused attention, a Level III pro can dramatically improve the lot for both sides of the equation.

The industry connection. The last area of professional engagement takes place outside of the organization, but is linked closely to those in your particular field. Industry organizations serve many functions, not the least of which is meeting peers and colleagues who share your passion for your chosen occupation. This allows benchmarking and idea sharing across company, organizational, cultural, and international lines. It also offers the opportunity for networking with like-minded individuals who face similar problems as well as exposing you to the latest ideas and experts from the field of interest. Here are a few guidelines as you engage with industry at large.

- **Pick one or two of the top organizations.** Organizations are like rabbits, they reproduce quickly. Some are genuinely interested in promoting the industry; others are shells for political agendas, or merely to produce revenue for the organization's directors. Any organization that has been around for ten years and is recognized by the mainstream of the industry is probably a safe bet. Another sanity check is that a good organization shouldn't cost an individual an arm and a leg to join. Industry dues are tax deductible (at least for now), but that doesn't excuse price gouging either for annual dues or to attend industry events such as seminars and conferences.

- **Once you are in, get involved.** Many professionals are satisfied with attending the annual conferences for networking purposes, but they miss a real opportunity to grow professionally while simultaneously helping the industry. Find a committee or sub-committee that needs a hand, and that you have a passion for, and then dig in. Be careful not to overextend by being clear from the beginning how much time and effort you can put into the volunteer position, and then hold your ground when they try to load you up—which they will if you are doing a good job.

- **Don't overlook local and regional organizations.** These are usually less expensive and much easier to engage with simply due to the geographical considerations. It also lets you keep an eye on the local competition and scout for new talent for your own organization. Again, take care to manage expectations so you avoid the twin demons of getting in over your head or disappointing your colleagues when the workload cranks up at the home or office.

If you are not already engaged at each of the four levels, take a few moments and map out a strategy to do so over the next year. Remember, deliberate practice involves planning for the specific purpose of improvement, and *professional engagement* is a perfect opportunity to get started.

Now, let's see where you perceive your current position with regards to *professional engagement* and consider a few more tools for moving forward.

Professional Engagement (10%) Self-assessment

For each of the following questions, grade yourself by circling 0, .5, or 1 in accordance with the following criteria.

0	.5	1
Almost Never	**Sometimes**	**Nearly Always**

I actively participate in one or more professional organizations.

0	.5	1

I voluntarily participate in my company's or organization's projects and programs that are not a part of my daily work requirements.

0	.5	1

I routinely participate in reporting systems, i.e., hazard reports, quality improvement suggestion programs, etc.

0	.5	1

I actively work to make others better at the individual level.

          0   .5   1

I have someone in my organization that I confide in and go to for advice and counsel without fear of retribution.

          0   .5   1

SUBTOTAL _____ x 2 = _____ (transfer this weighted score to the scorecard at the end of the book.)

Let's look at a few more tools for amping up our professional engagement skills.

Active participation

True masters of professionalism lean into tasks and relish the opportunity to engage with others in a collaborative fashion.

Roadblocks

- "Too busy" to participate due to competing priorities.
- Insecurity and fear of social interactions outside of your known personal and professional universe inhibit participation.
- Excuse making or demonizing the organization or program sponsor.

On ramps

- Join local and industry-wide professional organizations appropriate for your career and experience level.
- Participate in voluntary programs and projects within your organization.

- Take part in organizational or industry social activities and programs (i.e., softball team, golf outings, picnics, etc.).

Fast lanes

- Self-identify and willfully volunteer to participate in industry organizations and projects.
- Cheerfully and actively participate from day 1 of a project or team effort.
- Organize and launch team efforts for formal and informal activities.

Engagement is impossible without participation. Start small if you need to, but build this competency as a core part of your professionalism core.

Coaching and feedback

Remember the words of John Donne and fight to give and receive constructive feedback in a positive manner.

Roadblocks

- "Not my job" mindset inhibits teaching or helping others.
- Ego protection prevents active listening to others about your performance.
- Condescending attitude of "I know better, so listen to me" inhibits others from benefiting from your insights.

On ramps

- Routinely request feedback from all customers and coworkers to remediate or improve performance.

- Accept negative criticism gracefully and gratefully to promote future feedback.
- Remember to say "thank you" after receiving any tip or feedback, even if it is negative.

Fast lanes

- Work to make others better inside your organization as well as within your industry as a whole. Mentoring improves the mentor as much as the protégé, sometimes more.
- Initiate and engage in professionalism-related conversations with others to support continual professional and personal growth.

Feedback is the primary nutrient of deliberate practice. Everyone learns from everyone. Take your professionalism to the next level by sharing and learning with and from others.

Partnering

Building bridges across functional lines is time well spent, not only for your organizational effectiveness and efficiency, but as a down payment on the times when you will be the one in need.

Roadblocks

- "Us vs. them" mentality looks for advantages rather than cooperation.
- Unwillingness to collaborate across organizational boundaries.
- Grudging engagement outside of normal work groups only when required by superiors.

On ramps

- Remember to view both internal and external partners as *customers*, and hone your customer service skills every day.
- Look for opportunities to collaborate across organizational and functional professional boundaries to solve problems.
- Build good will by reaching across organizational lines to congratulate or thank others for a job well done.

Fast lanes

- Look for opportunities to assist those outside of your normal work group to build a "credit line" for times of need.
- Develop networks and build alliances <u>before</u> they are needed, inside and outside of the organization.

The best way to ensure you will get help when you need it is to voluntary offer yours when others need it. Pay it forward.

Reporting

Reporting is the lifeblood of formal feedback systems. Suggestion boxes and hazard reports are all too often ignored and not seen as a conduit for positive change.

Roadblocks

- Belief that reporting systems are "gotcha" programs that are punitive in nature.
- Perception that your input will not be acted upon or that nothing ever happens from field level input.

- Fear of being viewed as a "snitch" by peers for reporting information to management.

On ramps

- View reporting systems as a part of your job requirement and professional duty.
- Set a <u>conspicuous</u> positive example by routinely and visibly participating in all available reporting systems (i.e., hazard reports, quality programs, etc.).
- Encourage others to join you to make reporting systems more useful and robust.

Fast lanes

- Conduct personal research to improve personal awareness and the organization using reporting systems data.
- Work internally to make reporting systems transparent, nonpunitive, and responsive.

Level III professionals use the system to leverage both personal and organizational improvement. This is an easy one—if you have a reporting system, use it.

Summary

Professional engagement is where the rubber meets the road, and Level III professionals know how to provide world-class customer service, develop relationship-based networks, and build strong alliances inside and outside of the organization. Industry best practices are shared at these touch points, and your ability to influence learning and professional development in others happens here. In addition, the *application of professionalism* occurs inside this domain, so don't neglect this critical set of skills.

Now it's on to the fifth domain of professional excellence, *professional image*.

"To be yourself in a world that is constantly trying to make you something else is the greatest accomplishment."

Ralph Waldo Emerson

Chapter 10

Professional Image

Esse quam videri.[1]

"To be, rather than to seem to be."

Cicero

---

[1] Cicero. *On Friendship*. Ch 98.

"*Authenticity*; once you can fake that, you've got it made." This old salesman joke is definitely not what this chapter is about. While crafting an image is important, Cicero's quote *esse quam videri* reminds us that it is easier "to be, rather than to seem to be."

Level III professionalism <u>is</u> authentic, but a lifetime of habits that might be below the Level III threshold can be difficult to break. As we grow professionally, it is the perfect time to make sure our image does not betray what is happening inside.

When most people think about professional image, their thoughts immediately go to a "dress for success" mindset. In reality, what you wear and how you dress is only one small part of the professional image equation. We craft and sustain our professional image with every contact we make, including face-to-face meetings, phone calls, emails, instant messages, and social media participation. Sometimes, even what we <u>don't</u> do or say is a part of the image others form of us.

We will touch on all of these areas in this chapter, but first we need to address the breadth and depth of what creates our image. Some aspects of our professional image can be controlled by our actions, others are simply a part of who we are, but we need to be aware of their potential impact.

For example, I am a middle-aged, white American male of German descent with an accent that still hints I grew up in the Upper Peninsula of Michigan (think "Fargo"). In most business settings, this is not a concern. But with international clients, I must be aware of the potential for anti-American sentiment and the significance of my round eyes. In these settings, every gesture, posture, tone, and volume of voice is evaluated at some level. We can't pretend to be Chinese or Brazilian, but we can be aware of and *manage* our professional image for minimum distraction and maximum impact.

> "She believes that if you are not managing your own professional image, others will do it for you, and seldom to your advantage."

To a lesser extent, this same social dynamic plays out in different regions and organizational cultures in your own country. Working with the buttoned down types at the FBI is decidedly different than working with the more laid back crowd at Google. Military and ex-military types are big on protocol, others less so.

The bottom line is that your professional image communicates, interferes, attracts, and repels. At worst, we should manage our professional image to make it neutral. At best, our image communicates our Level III professionalism before we ever show up or say a word.

While professional image is only 10% of the Level III equation, it is a <u>critical</u> 10%. When it comes to professionalism, perception can be reality, at least to those looking in from the outside. Many people we work with have difficulty looking past our professional image to see what we are doing or hear what we are saying. For this reason alone, we must concern ourselves with perceptions, but remember that authenticity is the key to creating and sustaining a good impression.

Identity theft

Harvard Professor Laura Morgan Roberts specializes in helping others understand how to manage their professional image. She believes that if you are not managing your own professional image, others will do it for you, and seldom to your advantage. In an interview with the Harvard Business School, she lays it out this way.

> People are constantly observing your behavior and forming theories about your competence, character, and commitment, which are rapidly disseminated throughout your workplace. It is only wise to add your voice in framing others' theories about who you are and what you can accomplish.[1]

So how does one go about "adding their voice" to the ongoing dialog about who we are in the eyes of the world? It begins with understanding what others are looking for. Professor Morgan Roberts explains what most professionals hope to be seen as:

> Your professional image is the set of qualities and characteristics that represent perceptions of your competence and character as judged by your key constituents (i.e., clients, superiors, subordinates, colleagues). Most people want to be described as technically competent, socially skilled, of strong character and

---

[1] Stark, Mallory. *Creating a Positive Professional Image.* June 20, 2005. Found at http://hbswk.hbs.edu/item/4860.html

integrity, and committed to your work, your team, and your company. Research shows that the most favorably regarded traits are trustworthiness, caring, humility, and capability.[2]

That description sounds a lot like the *professional ethics, vocational excellence,* and *selflessness* pieces of Level III professionalism. If we are working to get better in each of those areas, all our professional image concerns should take care of themselves, right?

Not quite. Another way to look at it is to ask yourself what characteristics you <u>don't</u> want others to perceive.

Recall the *confirmation bias* trap, where we tend to look for evidence that supports what we want to see. If we turn the list around and ask ourselves how we can prevent perceptions of *untrustworthiness, self-importance, arrogance,* or *incompetence,* we are far more likely to be aware of our behaviors that might be interpreted negatively.

Experts call this skill set *impression management,* and it is extremely important for those of us who are busy climbing the professionalism ladder.

Build credibility, maintain authenticity

As we grow as professionals, it is natural that we take pride in our accomplishments, but it is equally important that we retain a sense of humility and remain true to ourselves and values. Most of us have seen fast trackers who change their personalities as they take

---

[2] Stark, Mallory. *Creating a Positive Professional Image.* June 20, 2005. Found at http://hbswk.hbs.edu/item/4860.html

on new titles, roles, and responsibilities. Technically, they may be gaining steam, but their credibility and authenticity are taking hits, crippling their professional image and effectiveness.

This is one of the major ways in which high potentials derail their careers. One senior executive who fell victim to this loss of authenticity put it this way. "Five years ago, I was making half of what I am today. But I look in the mirror and don't know who I am anymore. If I could, I would turn back the clock."[3]

There will always be tension between who you are and what others expect of you, but Level III professionals understand that if you don't remain true to your core values, it will eventually come back to bite you.

> "Most of us have seen fast trackers who change their personalities as they take on new titles, roles, and responsibilities. Technically, they may be gaining steam, but their credibility and authenticity are taking hits, crippling their professional image and effectiveness."

Speaking of things that can come back to bite you; let's talk about the perils of the internet, and specifically, social networking.

---

[3] Personal interview, February 2011.

"I'm so much cooler online"[4]

Country music recording artist Brad Paisley had a Number One hit in 2007 titled "Online." In it, he creates a new identity to boost his self-esteem. For most professionals, the problem is less about inventing new personas and more about sharing more actual personal information than is wise.

The issues surrounding the explosion of social media sites like *Facebook*, *MySpace*, and *LinkedIn* have business and government officials seriously concerned. More than a few individuals have lost their jobs and reputations as a result of what they decided to share online.

There appear to be two factors at work. The first is that employers and clients are looking more to the internet for information. The second factor is that people are just posting dumb stuff. The following data confirms the upward trend in both areas.

> According to a study by *Proofpoint*, an Internet security firm, of companies with 1,000 or more employees, 17% report having issues with employees' use of social media. And, 8% of those companies report having actually dismissed someone for their behavior on sites like *Facebook* and *LinkedIn*.[5]

Here are a few other statistics from the same study:

- 15% have disciplined an employee for violating multimedia sharing / posting policies

---

[4] "Online" is a single by American country music artist Brad Paisley from his 2007 album *5th Gear*. The single was Number One on the *Billboard* Hot Country Songs charts. In addition, the song's music video won a Video of the Year award for Paisley at the 2007 Country Music Association awards.

[5] Proofpoint study found at http://mashable.com/2009/08/10/social-media-misuse/

- 13% of US companies investigated an exposure event involving mobile or Web-based short message services
- 17% disciplined an employee for violating blog or message board policies

Let's look at a few examples, beginning with one of the most fundamental rules of social networking: *Don't disrespect your job, company, customers, or boss online*, especially if you have previously added them to your "friends" list, as in the sad but humorous case below.

> OMG! I HATE MY JOB!! My boss is a total pervvy wanker always making me do sh** just to piss me off!! WANKER!

This was posted at 6:03 PM to a young lady's *Facebook* page, likely just after she had returned from a tough day at work. It would be her last. At 10:53 PM her boss replied to her post.

> ... that 'sh** stuff' is called your 'job,' you know, what I pay you to do. But the fact that you seem to be able to f**k-up the simplest of tasks might contribute to how you feel about it. And last, you seem to have forgotten that you have two weeks left on your six month trial period. Don't bother coming in tomorrow. I'll pop your P45 (termination notice) in the post, and you can come in whenever to pick up any stuff you've left here. And yes, I'm serious.[6]

Here is rule two. *Consider ANYTHING you put online, or even in an email or text message to be available for the world to see.* Don't hit *post*, *comment*, or *send* until you have thought this aspect through.

---

[6] http://mashable.com/2009/08/10/social-media-misuse/

Here are a few other examples to drive this point home, all courtesy of the *Huffington Post* collection of employees who failed to understand that their internet identities were fair game for their employers to read and act upon.[7]

Swiss Woman Caught Surfing Facebook While 'Home Sick' From Work

According to Reuters, an employee of *Nationale Suisse* called out sick from work, claiming that "she could not work in front of a computer as she needed to lie in the dark." When she was discovered to be surfing *Facebook* from home, she was terminated. The woman maintained that she had used her iPhone to check her *Facebook* page from bed; however, *Nationale Suisse* issued a statement explaining that the incident "had destroyed its trust in the employee."

Virgin Atlantic Crew Members Insult Safety Standards, Passengers In Facebook Group

Virgin Atlantic took disciplinary action against 13 crew members who participated in a *Facebook* discussion that "criticised [Virgin's] safety standards and insulted passengers," according to the Guardian. The individuals "posted messages on *Facebook* referring to passengers as 'chavs' and making jokes about faulty engines," explains the Guardian, adding that they also "joked that planes were full of cockroaches and claimed the airline's jet engines were replaced four times in one year." The comments were promptly removed, the group was "sacked," and Virgin did not disclose many details other than a statement saying the unruly employees had "brought the company into disrepute."

---

[7] http://www.huffingtonpost.com/2010/07/26/fired-over-facebook-posts

Waitress Fired For Complaining About Customers

According to CBSNews, the waitress became irritated after she had to stay past her shift to wait on a table of two. When the table finally cleared out, they left what she deemed an inadequate tip. "Thanks for eating at Brixx," she reportedly wrote on her *Facebook* page, before using profanity and calling the customers "cheap." She later told UPI.com that she accepts responsibility for her actions but didn't expect to be fired over something she calls "very small." One of the restaurant's co-owners, however, said that she had violated company policy: "We definitely care what people say about our customers."

Grocery Store Fires Employees Because Of 'Derogatory' Facebook Group

Farm Boy, a Canadian grocery store chain, fired seven employees for creating a *Facebook* group ("I got Farm Boy'd") that mocked customers and included "verbal attacks against customers and staff." "No one was terminated for simply posting on a website," Farm Boy president Donny Milito told Canada.com, "We have always been about respecting our customers and employees. ... In the end I felt we had to stand up and defend ourselves in the best interest of our customers."

Remember the two basic rules: Don't disrespect anyone associated with your job and expect everything you put into an electron flow to surface at some point.

The "What happens in Vegas ... " myth

Although the social media explosion is a relatively recent phenomenon, similar events have been going on for years under the false impression that what one does away from home won't be discovered. This "what happens in Vegas stays in Vegas" mindset has never been less true than it is in today's electronically linked world where everyone has a cell phone camera and near instant access to the internet. The following example occurred in the summer of 2011 and involved two law enforcement patrol officers, both with more than 30 years of experience.

> Two Aurora police officers were pulled over near Torrington, Wyo., Wednesday evening after several people complained the officers were speeding with emergency lights activated and littering. The two officers were on their way to Rapid City, S.D., to attend the funeral of one of two police officers shot to death during a traffic stop on Aug. 2.
>
> Goshen County sheriff's Capt. Bryan Morehouse told 7NEWS one of the Aurora officers was ticketed on suspicion of driving while impaired, careless driving, and speeding. The second Aurora officer was cited for littering.[8]

Here are the basics of the situation. Two sworn officers of the law with decades of experience were driving an Aurora city police cruiser with a cooler of beer in the back, speeding through another state with their emergency lights on, and tossing refuse out the window. The driver tested to a .07 BAC which indicated he had likely been

---

[8] http://www.thedenverchannel.com/news/28838988/detail.html

consuming alcohol in the police vehicle, or shortly before departing (although no open containers were found in the car). The Aurora police spokesperson responded to the media:

> "We're embarrassed. We're in disbelief. It's quite a shock," Aurora Police Sgt. Cassidee Carlson told a local media outlet. "Complete embarrassment." A posting on the City of Aurora *Facebook* page said, "This is a tremendous embarrassment for the Aurora Police Department, and certainly not a reflection of the high standard of professionalism that we expect from our police officers. We are taking prompt and decisive action to gather all the facts and conduct a thorough investigation. These officers will be held accountable."[9]

The outcomes of any disciplinary actions were not yet available, but it is clear that one act of poor judgment put over 60 years of professional service at risk. In an increasingly linked and recorded world, no professional is really ever off duty.

A few basics

Let's turn our attention to a few simple rules of thumb for managing our professional image in all environments.

Appearance counts

Obviously, how you look is important. Coworkers, supervisors, peers, and customers naturally form opinions about you based upon your fitness and dress.

---

[9] http://www.thedenverchannel.com/news/28838988/detail.html

The baseline standard is *neat, clean,* and *well groomed.* For decades, image consultants have recommended that it is best to dress for the job you *want,* not the job you currently have. A professional appearance sets you apart from those who aren't overly concerned about projecting a professional image. Even on so-called "casual Fridays," take an extra few seconds in front of the mirror to make sure you are "squared away."

The fragrance factor

There are image concerns on both ends of this spectrum. Excessive use of perfumes or colognes can affect people with allergies and create an unpleasant situation for other employees or customers.

To protect against the attack of designer perfumes, many offices have gone to a "fragrance free" workplace. A standard policy statement might read something like this:

"The simple rule of thumb here is unless you are expecting an emergency call from the maternity ward, ignore the damn phone when interacting with a live person in a professional setting."

This is a fragrance free office. Thank you for not wearing any of the following: cologne, after shave lotion, perfume, perfumed hand lotion, fragranced hair products, and/or similar products. Our chemically-sensitive co-workers and clients thank you.

This is not just a matter of courtesy any longer, as the use of perfumes in the workplace has even been the subject of lawsuits. Even if your workplace does not have a policy, use common sense.

PROFESSIONAL IMAGE 237

There is also danger on the other end of the olfactory spectrum—body odor, bad breath, and tobacco and alcohol odors. These are not polite topics, but are certainly worthy of mention to potential Level III professionals.

The easiest path here is to take every preventative measure, and keep a stick of deodorant and a few breath mints handy for the unexpected breakdown of your car air conditioner or the "biggie green chili burrito" lunch at Madman Jose's.

Electronic etiquette

Professional image in the information age is evolving, but there are a few general rules that are beginning to stick.

- *Beware the Blackberry (or Droid, iPhone, Xoom, iPad, etc.)*

    There is nothing that says "you don't matter to me" quite as well as someone who interrupts a discussion or meeting to look at or answer a buzzing smart phone. The term *Crackberry* came to being to illustrate how addicting our electronic buddies can be. This subject will be covered in more detail in a section on active listening in the next chapter, but the simple rule of thumb here is unless you are expecting an emergency call from the maternity ward, *ignore the damn phone* when interacting with a live person in a professional setting.

- *Establish a communication "pecking order"*

    Information comes at a modern professional in more ways and through more channels than at any time in our history, and the potential for overlooking a response to a colleague or customer is an ever present threat.

According to business communications experts, there is a general "pecking order" when it comes to responding to different forms of communication.

> Email should be answered within 24 hours and a telephone call returned even sooner. Social networking site requests take the lowest priority. The order makes sense because a phone call or email seeks specific information from the one individual being contacted. Social networks come last because they are typically a wide-open forum where communication is less targeted at one individual.[10]

Keeping up with communication demands can be challenging, but Level III professionals will make it a priority. Become the person who will "always get back to you" in a timely and predictable manner.

Now that we've covered some important ground on how to create and sustain an authentic professional image, let's look at our self-assessment and *roadblocks, on ramps,* and *fast lanes*.

Professional Image—*Looking and acting the part* as you do the right thing right

Image alone will not make a professional. We have all seen "empty suits" who try to impress others through form over function. However, impressions are important, and a sloppy appearance or poor communication etiquette can often be seen as an indicator of

---

[10] http://www.forbes.com/2009/10/09/social-networking-etiquette-entrepreneurs-management-wharton.html

a lack of motivation or poor attention to detail. Keep in mind that people form impressions about you both on and off the job, and then use the following assessment and tools to drive improvement.

For each of the following questions, grade yourself by circling 0, .5, or 1 in accordance with the following criteria.

0	.5	1
Almost Never	**Sometimes**	**Nearly Always**

Professional Image (10%)

Regarding fitness and dress, I look the part of a professional on the job.

0   .5   1

I have respectful interactions with all and interact in a positive manner, even in difficult situations.

0   .5   1

I never take part in work "gossip sessions" or make disparaging remarks about supervisors, coworkers or customers.

0   .5   1

I "carry" myself professionally in the presence of others.

0   .5   1

I promote a positive public perception of my organization and industry through my conduct and behaviors off the job.

0   .5   1

SUBTOTAL _____ X 2 = _____ (transfer this weighted score to scorecard at the end of the book)

Now let's look at some action steps to improvement.

Fitness and dress

In 1979, rocker Joe Jackson released a single titled "Look sharp!" His lyrics speak to the 21st century workplace. *You gotta look sharp. You gotta have no illusions. Just keep going your way looking over your shoulder.*[11] Remember, people are always watching, and your appearance is one of the first ways they will form an opinion of your professionalism—or lack thereof.

Roadblocks

- "No one cares" mindset, resulting in frequent sloppy appearance, Dress or fitness level is inappropriate or below cultural norm.
- "I'm so good at my job that appearances don't matter."
- Lack of awareness of poor hygiene habits (fragrance factor, etc.)

On ramps

- Look sharp without busting the curve. Make sure your fitness and dress are exemplary for the culture, but not so much that it looks like you are showing off or out to embarrass others.
- Immaculate hygiene—showered, deodorized, clean clothes or uniform, well groomed.

Fast lanes

- Don't measure your appearance based on the job you have, but rather the job you want.

---

[11] http://www.lyricsfreak.com/j/joe+jackson/look+sharp_20072730.html

- When working with customers or contacts from outside your organization, show respect by dressing "one level up."
- Don't forget the deodorant and breath mints.

Your *continuous improvement* skills are a perfect complement for enhancing your fitness and appearance, as well as improving our next topic—*communications*.

Communications

Remember, everything you say communicates your professionalism, no matter what media you say it in. Rule 2—electronic communications are immortal.

Roadblocks

- Participates in or tolerates "trash talk" about coworkers or the organization.
- Inappropriate or sloppy use of email, social media, chat rooms, or other online communication channels.
- Fails to listen, just waits their turn to talk.
- "Crackberry" addiction communicates "you are not as important to me as my vibrating smart phone."

On ramps

- Communicate clearly and succinctly with a consistently positive outlook.
- Respond to emails and phone calls in a timely manner.
- Clarify vague statements, ask probing questions.

- Use appropriate communication techniques and channels (email etiquette, phone manners, etc.).

Fast lanes

- Work to improve your abilities in all communications channels (verbal, written, electronic, and nonverbal) to achieve desired outcomes.
- Learn and practice "attentive, active listening" and courtesy in all live conversations.
- Encourage, support, and promote the communications effectiveness of others.

Don't underestimate the amount of improvement that can be made to your professional image through communications. Take a strategic approach and spend some time to see where you can gain traction.

Bearing and behavior on and off duty

Emerson was on the mark when he said, "Who you are speaks so loudly I can't hear what you're saying." Be responsible for professional behavior in all settings.

Roadblocks

- "What I do on my own time is my business" is used as an excuse for inappropriate or unprofessional behavior off the job.
- "What happens in Vegas stays in Vegas" mindset that results in different rules of behavior for the home office and the road.
- "Multiple self" mentality creates different personas and rules for online behaviors and comments.

On ramps

- Behaviors on and off the job are congruent and based on positive and authentic professional values.
- Walk the talk. Actions in all settings reflect positively on the individual, organization, and profession.
- Assume that someone you care about is always watching, and set the best possible example.

Fast lanes

- Take a special pride in representing yourself, your organization, and your industry in thought, word, and deed.
- Master exemplary conduct and professional bearing as a matter of routine excellence, even when angry, under stress, or tired.
- Seek to mentor those who need assistance with their professional image in a tactful manner.

In increasing numbers, employees are being disciplined or fired for off duty behaviors. Keep your Level III professional mindset in play 24/7.

Final words on professional image

Remember the sage advice from Harvard Professor Laura Morgan Roberts who tells us that if we don't manage our professional image, someone else will. From the first greeting of the day, through answering your last email, people are forming opinions about your professionalism. Also keep in mind that in today's electronically connected world, things you say or do today online will likely have an impact for years to come, when someone hits a Google search and up pops your blog comment from ten years earlier.

Most critically, have a solid plan for improvement that stays true to your values. You can't fake *authenticity*—at least not for long.

Speaking of important values, it's time to move along to our last domain of professionalism—*selflessness*.

"For where you have envy and selfish ambition, there you find disorder and every evil."

James 3:16

Holy Bible, New International Version

Chapter 11

Selflessness

"We are all here on earth to help others. What I can't figure out is what the others are here for."

W. H. Auden

Selflessness can have a tremendous personal and professional advantage. This is less of an oxymoron than it sounds. The ability to get outside one's own ego and see the world from a servant perspective is tremendously valuable and a rare skill in most professionals. As the final domain of Level III professionalism, this chapter will serve to bridge between your career and its legacy. At the final turn of the road, we are all connected, and what a professional gives back to their company, industry, and the world at large is as important as anything we are likely to accomplish during our own careers.

Humility, intrapersonal intelligence, attentive listening, and *mentoring* are the topics we will be covering, the first three as a set up for the last, where we will spend the majority of our time and space in this chapter discussing how we pass the torch of Level III professionalism across generational gaps.

Benjamin Franklin's 13th virtue

After spending 200 plus pages convincing you of how powerful you can be as a Level III, it's time to discuss one of the major dangers that success imposes on any high achiever—ego control. We are certainly not the first who have had this challenge, as evidenced in this quote from Benjamin Franklin's autobiography:

> My list of virtues contain'd at first but twelve; but a Quaker friend having kindly informed me that I was generally thought proud; that my pride show'd itself frequently in conversation; that I was not content with being in the right when discussing any point, but was overbearing, and rather insolent, of which he convinc'd me by mentioning several instances; I determined endeavouring to cure myself, if I could, of this vice or folly among the rest, and I added *Humility* to my list, giving an extensive meaning to the word.[1]

This is the man who invented bifocals, swim fins, the *Franklin* Stove, lightning rods, the mechanical odometer, and the flexible urinary catheter. He is the man who formed the first "fluid theories of electrical fire" and coined the terms *battery, condenser, conductor,* and *positive/negative electrical charges,* all based on a set of experiments he did by flying a kite into thunderstorms. This is the man who accurately mapped the Atlantic Ocean Gulf Stream with floats, a time piece, and celestial navigation equipment while sailing back and forth to Europe as a *passenger* on a variety of ships. If Ben Franklin was able to accomplish a sense of *humility* with his list of accomplishments, it ought to be possible for the rest of us.

---

[1] http://www.ushistory.org/franklin/autobiography/page42.htm

Humility is the controller of pride run amok. It derives its meaning from the Latin *humus*, or "of the earth," an excellent metaphor for staying "grounded" amidst our daily successes. In the Buddhist tradition, humility is essential for freeing oneself from the vexations of the human mind as we ride the roller coaster of success and failure through our daily lives. The deliberate practice of humility opens our minds and allows us to accept that there is still a lot we do not know. It makes us teachable, and therefore, wiser.

Servant leadership

For a modern professional, keeping our pride in check is essential for *servant leadership*, where we lead best by serving those who follow. Servant leaders put their people and their organizations before themselves. They don't view employees as a means to an end; rather employees' happiness and satisfaction is an end they place high on their priority list.

Level III professionals are leaders, regardless of their job title or position within an organization. They lead by the power of their example. As high achievers, they drive themselves hard, and enjoy the satisfaction of doing their job well and the personal and organizational successes that flow from their hard work. This can be a trap where the ego begins to drive the train.

In her article *In praise of selflessness: Why the best leaders are servants*, journalist Leigh

> "The deliberate practice of humility opens our minds and allows us to accept that there is still a lot we do not know. It makes us teachable, and therefore, wiser."

Buchanan makes this point in her interview with two entrepreneurs who have been through the challenges of driving performance and maintaining humility.

> Ari Weinzweig and Paul Saginaw understand the challenges better than most. The co-founders of Zingerman's Community of Businesses have built their $30 million food, restaurant, and training company on servant leadership principles. In the process, they've wrestled with three paradoxes.
>
> - First, the higher you rise, the harder you must work for others; no kicking back in the Barcalounger of success allowed.
>
> - Second, although you hold formal authority over employees, you must treat them like customers and, when reasonable, do their bidding.
>
> - Third, when your desires and the needs of your organization conflict, your desires draw the low card.
>
> "It's a big change from the way we're socialized to think about success," says Weinzweig. "When you've put so much energy into getting to a leadership position, this is hard."[2]

Hard but essential, and even the massive intellect of Ben Franklin struggled with controlling his ego, as he indicates in this tongue-in-cheek observation from his autobiography.

> In reality there is perhaps not one of our natural passions so hard to subdue as pride. Disguise it, struggle with it, beat it down, stifle it, mortify it as much as one pleases, it is still alive,

---

[2] http://www.inc.com/magazine/20070501/managing-leadership_Printer_Friendly.html

and will every now and then peep out and show itself ... For even if I could conceive that I had completely overcome it, I should probably be proud of my humility.[3]

Franklin's observation demonstrates acute self-awareness, which leads us nicely into our next topic on selflessness—*intrapersonal intelligence*.

Intrapersonal intelligence—the importance of self-awareness

The concept of intrapersonal intelligence comes from Howard Gardner's groundbreaking work on multiple intelligences in his 1983 best seller *Frames of Mind: The Theory of Multiple Intelligences*.[4] Gardner contends that people with intrapersonal intelligence are acutely intuitive and skillful at deciphering their own feelings and motivations.

It might seem odd that self-awareness is a key to selflessness. But the ego is tricky, as Mr. Franklin intuitively grasped. Individuals who are more aware of their own emotional states, feelings, and motivations tend to recognize and respond to the trappings of success and can counter them before the ego or pride takes control of their thinking.

Awareness of self-absorption and ego are critical to the next essential attribute of selfless professionalism—*attentive, active, listening*. Before we can practice servant leadership, we must be able to clearly

---

[3] http://www.ushistory.org/franklin/autobiography/page42.htm
[4] Gardner, Howard. *Frames of Mind: The Theory of Multiple Intelligences*. New York: Basic Books. 1983.

understand the needs of those we are serving. This is especially true in the critical skill of mentoring, where the social dynamics of the mentor-protégé relationship are fragile.

Attentive, active, listening

One proven method for getting outside of oneself is to become actively involved in the needs, concerns, and interests of others. To practice this aspect of Level III professionalism, we need to master three important elements of active listening: *hearing, understanding,* and *responding* appropriately. Let's briefly look at each and how they impact your ability to fully engage with the conversation.

Hearing. This is the physical aspect of your ears receiving sounds. In today's active workplace, the use of cell phones, speaker phones, and multiplayer conference calls make this far more difficult than ever before. Make certain that you are minimizing interference, and position yourself appropriately and adjust volume levels to allow you to clearly hear the speaker. This seems like a no-brainer, but a few years ago after a conference call, I asked one of our team members what they thought of the customer's position on a topic. "I don't know," she responded, "I was down at the other end of the table and couldn't hear a word." When I asked why she didn't ask us to turn up the volume or move the speaker closer, she replied, "I didn't want to sound stupid." In a classic line of political incorrectness and non-servant leadership, one of her colleagues responded, "Well you sure do now."

Understanding. This is where your brain processes the words that you hear and adds meaning in the context of the entire conversation. Subtle elements of tone, sarcasm, humor, and other intricacies of the discussion are applied to grasp full meaning. Often, some aspects of the conversation will remain unclear, and good listeners will probe for deeper understanding.

Responding. Once you understand all or most of what you are hearing, the last piece of the equation is responding. This is the aspect of attentive listening where great listeners ask probing questions and make clarifying statements to ensure they were grasping both the intent and the facts of the discussion.

With these three basics under control, let's review the basic steps in the procedure of active listening as described by an industry expert in this area. Dr. Larry Alan Nadig is a clinical psychologist who works in the extreme communications world as a family and marriage counselor. He goes beyond the basics of eye contact and body posture to provide some valuable insights for real world attentive listening when the stakes are high, beginning with four common mistakes many professionals make in the listening process.[5]

- Avoid preoccupation; settle your mind on the task at hand, which is listening for *meaning*.
- Don't rehearse your response while pretending to listen.
- Fight the urge to judge or emotionally respond; listen non-judgmentally.
- Don't parrot back what you heard verbatim. It is often seen as pandering and disrespectful. Paraphrase what you thought you heard in your own words.

---

[5] http://www.drnadig.com/listening.htm

In addition to these areas to avoid, Dr. Nadig suggests the following tips to improve your attentive listening skills. Depending on the purpose of the interaction and your understanding of what is relevant, seek to understand:

- Accounts of the facts
- Thoughts and beliefs behind the speaker's words
- Feelings and emotions driving the intent of the message
- Expectations and hopes on how you will respond or act

A second key skill is to admit when you don't understand.

If you are confused, tell the person you don't understand, ask them to say it another way, or use your best guess. If you are incorrect, the person will realize it and will likely attempt to correct your misunderstanding.[6]

They will also realize you are actively listening.

Finally, know when to quit using active listening. Once you accurately understand the sender's message, re-engage with your normal communications style, but be prepared to go back into the attentive listening mode when the need arises.

Professionals act on the basis of their understanding, but misunderstandings still occur all too frequently. With active listening, if a misunderstanding has occurred, it will be known immediately and can be clarified before any further damage occurs.

The deliberate practice of humility and attentive, active listening are all skills required for the most important role a Level III professional can undertake in the pursuit of selfless professionalism—mentoring.

---

[6] http://www.drnadig.com/listening.htm

What is a mentor?

The word "mentor" originated in the book *The Odyssey*. Odysseus had a close friend named *Mentor* who in his old age cared for Odysseus' son *Telemachus* during the Trojan War. For a period, the goddess *Athena* took the form of Mentor, and encouraged his development in many areas as well. Throughout, "Mentor embodied male and female qualities such as being nurturing, supportive, and protective as well as aggressive, assertive, and risk taking. Mentor acted in the role of parent, teacher, friend, guide, and protector."[7]

Mentoring is a tool that organizations and individuals use to nurture and grow their human resources. It can be an informal practice or a formal program. With regards to professionalism, it may be the most important tool in the arsenal, as it has the potential to cross generational lines to promote the six domains of professional excellence.

Informal mentoring

Most experienced professionals are involved in several informal mentoring relationships and don't even recognize them as such. Every time a high performing professional accomplishes a task as a part of a team or conducts an after-action debrief in the presence of a coworker, mentoring is taking place. Yet, there is an elevated level of interest and engagement between colleagues that typically form a mentoring relationship.

---

[7] Jeruchim, Joan; & Shapiro, Pat. *Women, Mentors, and Success*. New York: Jawcett Columbine, 1992.

It may start with someone asking a simple question, such as "You've been around a while, what's up with this new vacation policy?" or "Why does Janet do this differently than you do?" This type of question lets you know that the colleague respects your opinion and views you as someone they can trust.

From here, the relationship often leads to a deeper engagement across multiple topics. Even though the relationship remains informal, there are three typical functions an informal mentor uses to add value to their interactions.

Communicator. A good mentor is easy to talk to and will go out of their way to encourage two-way communication on important topics. They will make themselves available as a sounding board for ideas or concerns. They will also know how to reign in out-of-bounds communications, such as workplace gossip, disrespectful comments about the company or coworkers, or any comments of a race, gender, or sexual nature. In short, a good mentor establishes a relationship where open interaction can take place with a target towards improvement.

Advisor. As an *advisor*, an informal mentor builds on the trust established in the *communicator* role to nudge the improvement agenda forward. He or she works with their colleague to identify career-related skills, interests, and values, and assists them in evaluating career options and strategies. Additionally, an advisor is always alert for pitfalls and obstacles that can derail a protégé's progress. Finally, an advisor adds the salt of reality to all career-related discussions, not to dampen enthusiasm, but to protect against disillusionment.

Advocate. The final role for an informal mentor is as an *advocate*. Active advocacy occurs when the relationship has progressed to the point where the mentor feels it is in the best interest of the company and the mentored colleague to move them forward. In this role, the mentor might recommend training, new positions, or projects as developmental opportunities. One has to be careful here, or they can be perceived as becoming a *sponsor* or *protector*. These roles exceed the traditional limits of informal mentorship.

There are also some important items to consider when seeking an appropriate professionalism mentor. Let's quickly review a few.

> "A good mentor can assist you in all six domains of professionalism, and they can do it from the perspective of having operated in your environment. Their hindsight can be your foresight."

Keys for those seeking mentorship

Some might ask *how can seeking a mentor help achieve selflessness*? The answer to that question is critical to understanding Level III professionalism. First, a good mentor can assist you in all six domains of professionalism, and they can do it from the perspective of having operated in your environment. Their hindsight can be your foresight. This will make you improve faster and be more productive for your company and peers, which is most assuredly a selfless act. Secondly, a good mentor will help you prepare to be a mentor for others. This generation-to-generation "passing of the torch" is how we create the future of professional excellence. It's how we give something back.

The first essential in seeking mentorship is that you want to find someone who will make you better. This may sound obvious, but there are many Level I professionals out there who seek out "mentors" who will tolerate, and even validate, their casual attitude towards compliance and professionalism. Don't make this mistake.

Finding the right mentor is important, but don't obsess about finding Yoda, Mr. Miyagi, or Gandalf. Get started with someone you respect and trust, and you can continue to seek other mentors. In point of fact, it is your personal attitude towards the relationship that is the most critical aspect for success. Here are a few guidelines, beginning with how to open the door.

> "There are many Level I professionals out there who seek out 'mentors' who will tolerate, and even validate, their casual attitude towards compliance and professionalism."

There are a few experts out there that suggest the best way to secure a mentor is to simply approach them and ask "Will you be my mentor?" To me, this is just a bit too bold, and if not done gracefully, could be a little bit creepy in a stalker kind of way. I say look for your mentor through the normal activities of your job and be ready when the opportunity presents itself.

Do something professional to get their attention. This could be something as simple as volunteering for a project or assisting with a difficult task. If by chance your potential mentor approaches you to offer advice, help, or congratulations, that makes it that much easier. Start simple by asking their opinion or advice on something you want to know more about. Let the relationship grow from there.

Don't expect too much too early. People are busy, and it is likely that the kind of person you respect and admire is already shouldering a heavy load. Recognize and respect this by prefacing questions with something like: "I know you are busy, but do you have time for a short discussion on ... It shouldn't take more than 10 minutes." Don't be surprised if they offer more time than you asked for.

Be prepared when your new mentor wants to engage. If your mentor makes time for you, be ready and, unless it's impossible, take advantage of every opportunity. Being prepared means more than showing up, so have a "next time we talk plan" in your back pocket.

Make the relationship beneficial for your mentor. Occasionally, your advisor will ask for your help. Give it if you can and make sure you do a bang up job of whatever it is. Look for other opportunities to give back, such as keeping an eye out for articles of interest to them, or talking them up in front of others.

Don't forget who helped you. If a mentorship relationship works, it is natural for the protégé to pass the mentor at some point on their way up the career ladder. Remember to thank them formally and speak of their assistance publicly. If you ever have a chance to reciprocate by lending a helping hand to someone they care about, don't pass up the opportunity to do so.

> "To drive Level III professionalism forward, formal mentor programs must find and train the best possible candidates."

Level III professionalism is new, rigorous, and tremendously empowering. These factors may suggest a move to a more formalized form of mentorship program.

Formal mentor programs

For mentorship to be effective in promoting professionalism, we must move beyond the traditional "experience is the best teacher" mindset to formally prepare both the prospective mentors and their *paired professional* (sounds so much better than "protégé) for the rigors of Level III professionalism.

Attributes of a formal mentor

To drive Level III professionalism forward, formal mentor programs must find and train the best possible candidates.

The most critical prerequisite for professional mentors is the authentic desire to be one. Many resist the mentorship role for reasons that can be easily overcome with a bit of explanation and training. Much of the reluctance stems from fear of the unknown, and as programs are developed to provide structure and relevance, these fears should dissipate. Although the desire to mentor is important, a "volunteer only" approach will probably not yield the best pool of candidates. Rather than looking exclusively for volunteers, the best means of selecting prospective mentors is to look for the following qualities, and then provide them with a set of tools that will ensure their success. Most viable candidates will lower their guard once they know they are being provided the training and tools for success. Here is a short list of qualifications to look for.

Good mentors will:

- Genuinely care about the development of their paired professional as well as their own personal legacy as they view retirement from their profession at some point in the future.

- Understand and be up to date on the core principles of Level III professionalism. You can't hope to teach what you don't know, and a lack of depth is a recipe for failure.

- Have time and energy to put into the mentorship relationship.

- Embrace the concept of deliberate practice and be able to explain its value and relevance in the environment where the paired professional will be working.

- Practice and communicate authentic humility. This is often best accomplished by sharing both failures and success stories from their experience.

- Look to learn as well as teach. Good students never stop learning, and by role modeling the *continuous improvement* aspects of Level III professionalism, both sides of the equation benefit.

- Be good storytellers and have good stories to tell. This goes well beyond "there I was" stories, and must include relevant lessons. This skill is easily learned with a bit of practice and preparation.

- Be genuinely respectful of the company, coworkers past and present,

> "If we hope to change the professionalism culture of an organization or industry, we have to prepare a vanguard of certified professionalism mentors. I like to call this group of world changers *Going Pro Ninjas*. We need them now, and we need them in large numbers."

- and his industry. A successful mentor must also respect the confidentiality of the paired professional and understand the limits of that confidentiality.

- Be open to change. Mentors must embrace changes within the organization they serve and communicate the need for their paired professional to do the same.

- Be patient. Mentorship relationship bonds form slowly, and benefits take time. Setbacks are frequent.

Seldom will someone be available with all of these desirables. However, the selection process can be made more predictable through selection instruments and expert interviewing techniques.[8]

What we can't select for, we must train, and train seriously.

Professional Mentor Certification: The next logical step

Mentorship of professionalism is far more than finding an experienced person with a good track record and asking them to pass along the party line. If we hope to change the professionalism culture of an organization or industry, we have to prepare a vanguard of certified professionalism mentors. I like to call this group of world changers *Going Pro Ninjas*. We need them now, and we need them in large numbers.

Towards that end, we have created a one-week intensive program to train and certify new mentors in the art and science of Level III professionalism, as well as the core skills of mentorship. The first of

---

[8] For more information on these tools, contact Convergent Performance at http://www.convergentperformance.com

SELFLESSNESS 265

these programs was created for the aviation industry, which faces a critical demographic shift in the next 3-5 years. The program is called *Generations in Aviation* and provides the complete package of knowledge, tools, and inspiration to develop world-class mentors, as well as the next generation of world-class aviation professionals.

The formal certification program provides two-way survey instruments, personal professionalism inventories, and dozens of interpreted case studies and is meant to be focused, edgy, actionable, and resourced—or what we call the professional mentor's FEAR factor. The goal of the *Generations in Aviation* program is to tie all aviation professionals to the legacy of excellence that has been a part of the aviation industry since Orville told Wilbur to meet him at the bicycle shop to talk about a new idea.

Generations in Aviation Formal Mentor Certification Program

The Latin tag line *Omnia Mea Mecum Porto* means "All I have I carry with me," and represents the responsibility and accountability that goes with the profession.

Customized programs for other industries and organizations are being created around the same principles as the *Generations* professional mentor certification.

Mentorship—formal or informal—represents the epitome of selflessness. By giving the gift of professionalism to the next generation, we enhance their abilities to grow and continue to prosper in uncertain economic times.

Now let's take a quick self-assessment to increase our personal awareness of our state and readiness for Level III *selflessness*.

Selflessness—<u>Helping others and the world</u> by doing the right things right

One of the doors to high performance opens outward. Those who perform for someone or something outside of themselves often find motivation and energy that continuously drive professional growth.

For each of the following questions, grade yourself by circling 0, .5, or 1 in accordance with the following criteria.

0	.5	1
Almost Never	**Sometimes**	**Nearly Always**

Selflessness (10%)

I enjoy seeing someone else get credit for a job well done.

0	.5	1

SELFLESSNESS

I view my organization's priorities ahead of my own self-interest.

           0   .5   1

I role model the ideal of "service before self" in my daily work activities.

           0   .5   1

I get as motivated by the opportunity to help someone else as I do to further my own career or personal agenda.

           0   .5   1

I willingly put in extra time and effort to complete tasks, even when I am not required to so.

           0   .5   1

SUBTOTAL _____ X 2 = _____ (transfer this weighted score to scorecard at the end of the book)

Now let's look at some action steps for improvement, and check these items as you seek higher levels of service.

Service motivation

Adopting a "servant leader" mindset opens your mind to the needs and perceptions of others, which is critical for personal improvement.

Roadblocks

- Narcissism that says "I know better than anyone what needs to be done here," blocks feedback or open communication.

- "Me first" or "they owe me" attitude creates conditions where your personal agenda is obvious in team or organizational activities.
- Refusal to engage with those who have no personal advantage to offer you.

On ramps

- Rational balance between internal and external motivations that favors service to others over personal agendas.
- Ensure that actions meet organizational needs; align organizational objectives and public interests.
- Don't seek or expect praise or favors in return for good work.

Fast lanes

- Roll model and champion the ideal of "service before self."
- Volunteer for altruistic projects for their own sake, and not for what's in it for you.
- Assist others when it is inconvenient and hard, not just when it is convenient and easy.

A service-oriented mindset takes a bit of work to develop, especially when you are already extremely busy. But try and leverage in a few volunteer projects, and you will see the rewards.

External focus

Concentration and focus are key traits of Level III professionals. If not guarded against, this can lead to an internal focus that excludes the agenda or concerns of others.

Use the following tips to fight this tendency.

Roadblocks

- "Careerist" mindset that views others as tools for personal advancement.
- Worldview that runs through a "what's in it for me" (WIIFM) filter.
- Lack of time or energy to look beyond your current tasks.

On ramps

- Find a small way to demonstrate a commitment to serve others, the organization, and the public at large.
- Learn to recognize the WIIFM filter and respond with a "what can I do for you?" mindset.
- "Lighten up" your serious attitude to enjoy the presence and conversation of others.

Fast lanes

- Begin to sacrifice your time, energy, and if necessary, personal agenda for the good of others and the organization.
- Give something back to the organization, industry, and people who have made your career possible.
- Find someone to mentor.

External focus opens your heart and mind to the world around you. Success in that extended world becomes much easier and more rewarding if you can learn the virtue of humility.

Humility

Author and philosopher C.S. Lewis once wrote that "a man who is eating or lying with his wife or preparing to go to sleep in humility, thankfulness, and temperance, is, by Christian standards, in an infinitely higher state than one who is listening to Bach or reading Plato in a state of pride."[9]

Use the following tools to assess and elevate your humility.

Roadblocks

- Pride that says "look at me" after every success.
- Inability to see the hand of others or God in our success.
- Extreme partisanship that won't allow credit to those with whom we disagree with.

On ramps

- Develop a mindset of gratitude for all the opportunities and gifts you have been given.
- Develop a modest, realistic opinion of your own importance.
- Share your accomplishments in a modest, positive way when requested or necessary.

Fast lanes

- Allow your record, actions, and peers to speak for you regarding your successes.
- When you *must* speak of your credentials, frame it in a way that remains focused on what you can do for others as a result of these talents.

---

[9] http://www.quotedb.com/quotes/345

SELFLESSNESS

Humility; intrapersonal intelligence; attentive, active listening; and mentoring are the cornerstones of *selflessness* for the Level III professional. Work these areas along with the other five domains of professionalism and you will see dramatic improvement in your performance. Just don't be too prideful when it happens!

We conclude this chapter with a *Blue Threat proverb* that speaks poignantly to the challenge and reward of helping others.

Harness the Merlin Effect[10]

Merlin was the wizard to King Arthur. Merlin's imperative wasn't to make himself the world's greatest wizard; it was to make Arthur the best king. Ironically, as you seek to make others better, you don't slow your own improvement efforts—you actually accelerate them. It has long been known that the best way to learn is to teach, so as you apply the tools of Level III professionalism to control your errors and pursue precision, strive to lift those around you by your example and your support.

As Gandhi said, be the change you want to see in the world.

---

[10] With many thanks to Dale Condit, who taught me the *Merlin Effect* metaphor in a world-class Program Management training course at the USAF Academy in 1998.

"I want a pit crew. I hate the procedure I currently have to go through when I have car problems."

Dave Barry, Journalist

Chapter 12

Tying In the New Professionalism: Approaches that Work

"When we blindly adopt a religion, a political system, a literary dogma, we become automatons. We cease to grow."

Anais Nin

TYING IN THE NEW PROFESSIONALISM

The success of any innovation rests upon it not being <u>too</u> new.

While professionalism is definitely personal, it must also be inclusive of related efforts. We can do much on our own, but at times we need the pit crew, as Dave Barry so eloquently puts it.

Smart people have been thinking about human performance for thousands of years, and only a fool would ignore things that are working in favor of relying exclusively on something they just read in a new book—even one as good as this one. For that reason, we must tie into the web of systems that are already working, as well as point out how a rising tide of *professionalism* lifts all boats. Towards that end, let's dig into a few complementary approaches that are currently working to improve human performance, and point out how Level III professionalism supplements or complements these initiatives.

Four traditional strategies on augmenting human performance

Over the past half-century, four primary strategies to improving human performance in the workplace have emerged. Each has been at least partially successful, and each has supporters, many of whom border on zealotry in their support for the independent use of their chosen position. Each in its own way seeks to control human variability. All link to professionalism in one way or another. Let's take a quick look at the philosophy, strengths, and weaknesses of each traditional strategy.

Technology—machines to the rescue

From the moment the first humanoid discovered how to use a tree limb as a lever or rock as a weapon, we have been tool makers, and there is little doubt that western society burns incense at the altar of the "technology solution." From anti-skid brakes to Lasik eye surgery, machines have extended and enhanced our ability to perform miraculous feats with ease and relative safety. But technology is not a miracle cure for all things and there is a dark side to the cult of mechanization. As hardware and software systems are built and integrated to assist, correct, monitor, or outright replace the human element, something evil this way comes.

Relaxed vigilance and the atrophy of our gray matter engines of ingenuity are a direct byproduct of a world where we seldom need to think, thanks to our perfectly logical silicon-based buddies. In aviation, we have given a specialized term to the tendency for humans to hand over responsibility to the machine—*primary-*

TYING IN THE NEW PROFESSIONALISM 277

backup inversion. A classic example of this is a simple altitude-alerting device that was originally designed to <u>remind</u> the pilot that he or she was approaching an intended altitude. These devices quickly became the primary alerting device as pilots found they no longer had to personally monitor the altitude of their aircraft until they heard the device go off. A more familiar example might be the over-reliance of drivers on GPS navigation systems. We may well be the last generation that is taught to read a highway road map.

As a young man growing up in the rural west of Michigan's Upper Peninsula, rarely a day went by when we did not have to find a solution to an interesting challenge. Out of necessity, we learned to manufacture parts as well as tools, lay and check trap lines, smoke fish, split firewood, clean and repair woodstoves, and a host of other creative thinking and doing chores. Because there were limited resources and more work than there was time to accomplish it, we got creative, we got efficient. I suspect that this was the case throughout most of human history up until the industrial revolution. But few grow up in this mentally challenging environment any more, making us all too ready to relinquish our thinking to software whenever and wherever we can.

> "Technology is not a miracle cure for all things and there is a dark side to the cult of mechanization. As hardware and software systems are built and integrated to assist, correct, monitor, or outright replace the human element, something evil this way comes."

To fill the thinking challenge void, we have manufactured mental games like *Sudoku* and *Brain Teasers* to keep our attention and neural pathways firing at some minimum level. For our youth, it is the video game, and I have to admit, there are some pretty cool ones out there that provide strategic and tactical thinking challenges. The point is that the world doesn't provide the mental challenges it once did, thanks in large part to computer-assisted everything. When the silicon chips stop working, sometimes we are not ready to mind the gap.

Beyond the loss of vigilance and creative thought capacity, another inherent weakness of the technology approach is that advanced automation brings its own set of problems. This has led to a relatively new science known as the human-machine interface (HMI). Learning how to communicate with highly sophisticated systems in high risk environments has led to some breakthroughs by contemporary human factors innovators.

> "The point is that the world doesn't provide the mental challenges it once did, thanks in large part to computer-assisted everything. When the silicon chips stop working, sometimes we are not ready to mind the gap."

One such breakthrough is *Automation Airmanship*®, a new aviation science that merges traditional flying skills with the ability to "elegantly manage and merge the unique and complementary capabilities of the man and machine."[1] A detailed breakdown of new information, skills, and observable behaviors has been compiled into a trainable curriculum that far exceeds anything currently taught elsewhere.

---

[1] Chris Lutat, author of *Automation Airmanship*, forthcoming 2012.

While the technology solution is far and away the leader in traditional approaches to managing human variability, there is a second place qualifier; those who see *process* and *organizational structure* as the solution.

Systems approaches—structure and process

Ever since Peter Senge of MIT published his seminal work on systems approaches, titled *The Fifth Discipline: The art and science of the learning organization*,[2] the world has gravitated towards greater levels of systems thinking. This was a much-needed advance at a time when public and private organizations were trying to find equilibrium following the dramatic growth of the 1980s and just in time for the dot com explosion. Senge argued for many of the same things other organizational management experts had advocated, such as the need for a shared vision, mastery of vocational skills, the use of mental models to align goals, and teamwork. Unlike his predecessors, professor Senge took the critical additional step of explaining how all of these essentials were tied together through the *fifth discipline* of systems thinking. It is no surprise that systems advocates have built upon this model.

In the arena of industrial safety, *safety management systems*, or SMS, are the current rage. The general philosophy of the SMS approach is that most organizations can be better structured and aligned to support the safety agenda. Inside the SMS, *process* is king operating

---

[2] Senge, Peter M. *The Fifth Discipline*, Doubleday/Currency. 1990

behind multiple defensive layers of organizational structure. This is the so-called "Swiss Cheese" model made famous by Professor James Reason in his seminal work *Human Error*.[3]

> "Senge himself pointed out a major 'learning disability' in many organizations was the fact that people fail to recognize their purpose as a part of the enterprise."

Reason's approach has been amplified by the work of Professors Douglas Wiegmann and Scott Shappell through the *Human Factors Analysis and Classification System*[4] (HFACS), a detailed system to analyze incidents, accidents, and events to pinpoint human factors contributors.

SMS is a formal, top-down business approach to managing risk, which includes the necessary organizational structures, accountabilities, and policies. According to one standard set by the U.S. Government, a good SMS is composed of four functional components: *Safety policy, safety risk management, safety assurance,* and *safety promotion*.

The strengths of this approach are many, including the robust nature of data collection and use, as well as clarifying authorities and accountabilities among management officials. Level III professionals will clearly recognize the value of quantifiable improvement and are likely to be champions of reporting and analysis.

The weakness of the systems approach is that its top-down approach seemingly discounts both the positive value and negative

---

[3] Reason, James. *Human Error*. Cambridge University Press. 1990
[4] Wiegmann, D.A. & Shappell, S.A. The Human Factors Analysis and Classification System (HFACS): Report No. DOT/FAA/AM-00/7. Federal Aviation Administration, 2000; or Wiegmann, D.A. & Shappell, S.A. *Applying Reason: the human factors analysis and classification system* (HFACS): Human Factors and Aerospace Safety I(I), 59-86, 2001

performance aspects of the individual. Senge himself pointed out a major "learning disability" in many organizations was the fact that people fail to recognize their purpose as a part of the enterprise. Instead, they see themselves as an inconsequential part of a system over which they have little influence, leading them to limit themselves to the jobs they must perform at their own positions. Level III professionals will both lift and challenge systems approaches.

A subset of the systems approach that also deserves appropriate merit and scorn is rooted in standardization and proceduralization, our next topic of attention.

Proceduralization—reliability through standardization

Although some may see this as a subset of the systems approach, the rise of regulation and proceduralization over the past few decades has been legion, and in some cases detrimental to the systems they purport to serve. Proceduralization rests on the supposition that there are certain "do's and don'ts" that are so foundational that they must be mandated.

The approach is rooted in the work of Herbert William Heinrich, an analyst working in the insurance industry in the 1930s who discovered that the vast majority[5] of workplace injuries were caused

---

[5] In the 1930s, Heinrich reviewed thousands of accident reports completed by supervisors and from these drew the conclusion that most accidents, illnesses, and injuries in the workplace are directly attributable to "man-failures," or the unsafe actions of workers. Of the reports Heinrich reviewed, 73% classified the accidents as "man-failures;" Heinrich himself reclassified another 15% into that category, arriving at the still-cited finding that 88% of all accidents, injuries, and illnesses are caused by worker errors. Source: SEMCOSH Fact Sheet, 2004.

by human error. This initial analysis set the stage for decades of research that has evolved into various forms and levels of workplace injury, accident, and error analysis. Two of the longest lasting approaches have become known as *behavior-based safety* and *human reliability* approaches.

"Some industries, such as nuclear power and aviation, have embraced proceduralization and standardization to the degree that a team of individuals who have never met can perform at the same levels as teams that have been together for years."

The general philosophy in both of these approaches is that a trained observer can spot and correct performance problems and, over time, this will lead to sufficient data which can be used to identify at risk locations or events and standardize behaviors in the workplace appropriate for the environment and tasks. These standardized bits of guidance typically take the form of procedures.

There are many advantages to this approach. The first is that procedures can be trained, communicated, and observed with great standardization. They create a "right way" to do things. In many high risk environments, procedures are a necessary "if-then" link that ensures good outcomes. Some industries, such as nuclear power and aviation, have embraced proceduralization and standardization to the degree that a team of individuals who have never met can perform at the same levels as teams that have been together for years. Other industries, such as health care, are just beginning to recognize the value and have a long way to go.

The Quality Assurance (QA) connection

Another advantage to standardized procedures is that trained quality assurance personnel can evaluate and correct in real time in the local setting. Level III professionals will make excellent observers in this role as they will already possess both the observational skills and an appreciation of the data-driven approach in the local environment. Depending on the seriousness of the effort, QA can result in rigorous data analysis and face-to-face interactions between a qualified observer and workers who understand both the context and consequences of the proposed procedure. Advanced human reliability techniques include detailed task analyses cross referenced with failure rates for part and whole tasks. This approach, called the *probabilistic risk analysis* (PRA) model, is currently on the cutting edge of quantifiable techniques.

But there are also several professionalism risks associated with too much reliance on written procedure.

The first is *over-proceduralization*. Much like over reliance on technology, if we reduce human performance to merely a series of "see this, do that" procedures, we are limiting both the vigilance and initiative of the human element. A second risk is that in some environments, over-proceduralization often leads to noncompliance as workers find

> "Some feel another weakness of the behavior-based approach is that by isolating the performance equation to workplace behaviors, underlying personal factors are minimized."

shortcuts and workarounds to "get the job done" outside the lines. The new professionalism addresses these compliance issues head on under both *professional ethics* and *vocational excellence*.

Some feel another weakness of the behavior-based approach is that by isolating the performance equation to workplace behaviors, underlying personal factors are minimized. For example, a worker who is preoccupied or distracted by off duty concerns might commit errors or safety-related behaviors that result in data about a particular activity or location, when neither the activity nor location was causal or even relevant to the true precursor for the mistake. Level III professionalism training should help, as the 3D approach is specifically designed to combat this type of complacency.

Finally, some experts argue that the dichotomy of classifying an action as "correct" or "incorrect" for the situation or event is a gross oversimplification of a complex phenomenon. This is one of the primary areas of resistance in the health care industry, where many surgeons push back against what they perceive is an attempt to create "cookbooks" of procedures for complex operations with too many variables to predict, let alone plan for and proceduralize.

While the strength of a data-based strategy is in its numbers, it is also a weakness for individuals who may be outliers from the statistical norm on a given day or task. Level III professionals are taught to recognize this personal drift, when they may not be firing on all cylinders and potentially at risk, and this competency should strengthen the value of any procedural approach.

The final area to tie into is one of the most important, because in the modern workplace, few work alone.

Communication solutions—quality through teamwork

Over the past 30 years, a variety of human performance approaches have emerged from a central theme—*none of us is as smart as all of us*. The first challenge was getting anyone to listen.

Throughout most of the 20th century, the world was the home of the larger-than-life leader. Self-made men with giant egos, military generals, and corporate raiders. Think George Patton, Douglas MacArthur, and John Wayne. If they wanted your opinion, they would beat it out of you.

But the free market has a way of taming big egos through innovation and competition. I'm not sure when it started, but visionaries like Norman Vincent Peale and Edward Deming figured out the competitive advantages of less dictatorial forms of communication and influence, and a new generation of collaboration was born. Level III professionals work best in environments where their *professional engagement* skills can be lent to collaborative efforts.

Almost overnight, from executive boardrooms to the cockpits of commercial aircraft, the authority gradient was flattened in an attempt to reduce intimidation and foster greater teamwork. From these beginnings, multiple spinoffs were born to train the advantage.

Commercial aviation has led this charge and developed what may be the most well-known and successful of these programs—*Crew Resource Management* (CRM). CRM has evolved from what was initially a communications-focused effort on getting overbearing airline Captains to listen to their crews into a robust multifaceted toolkit. Modern versions of CRM teach such complex skills as threat and error management (TEM) and situational awareness (SA) during time compressed crisis situations. CRM is trained in the classroom and simulators and is evaluated on every pilot's initial and recurring check ride. Perhaps the most famous event demonstrating the efficacy of CRM was the near miraculous recovery of United Airlines Flight 232.

United Flight 232 was a scheduled flight of a DC-10 from Denver to Chicago on July 19, 1989. Enroute, the crew experienced catastrophic failure of the tail-mounted engine. The manner in which the engine failed resulted in high-speed shrapnel being hurled from the engine, penetrating the hydraulic lines of all three independent hydraulic systems on board the aircraft, resulting in the loss of all flight controls. Despite these losses, the crew was able to attain and then maintain limited control by using the only systems still workable: the two remaining engines. Utilizing their experience and ingenuity to keep the aircraft in the air, the crew evaluated and tested all options for getting the aircraft back on the ground. Close coordination with air traffic control, the flight attendants, and rescue personnel resulted in the crew being able to get the aircraft on the ground in a controlled crash landing. Although 111 fatalities resulted, 184 others owe their lives to the ability of the crew to use their training to accomplish what many believed was impossible.

In the aftermath of the event, Captain Al Haynes specifically credited CRM training for the manner in which the crew was able to perform.

The general philosophy of the CRM strategy is that teams will outperform individuals in nearly all situations if they are trained to do so. Additionally, individuals trained in this manner can perform at high levels under extreme conditions even when they have not worked together before—as was the situation with United 232.

But teamwork alone will not overcome failures of professionalism. Even in the airlines where advanced forms of CRM are now mandatory, we have seen multiple failures where breakdowns in professionalism have led to embarrassing and sometimes tragic outcomes. A second weakness is that many bright individuals do not perform well in teams. There is also the inconvenient fact that the world often throws us challenges when we are forced to act alone, either due to time constraints or because team options are not available.

While these four strategies are certainly not the only advances made in human performance circles, they represent the primary focus of modern industries continuing struggle to optimize human performance.

A contemporary integrated approach—professional growth with the resources at hand

One limitation that all of the previous strategies have in common is that they cannot be done by a single individual operating independently without additional outside resources. The advanced technology approach requires, well, advanced technology. Systems and procedural strategies require you to be a part of a functional system that provides structure, process, and procedures. To a lesser extent, communications strategies require some training in group dynamics and communications tools.

The Blue Threat/Going Pro (BT/GP) strategy can be done anywhere, by anyone with the will to improve and an ability to provide oneself with objective feedback. Furthermore, the new professionalism has been specifically designed to integrate with other traditional performance strategies like the ones described above. However, there are dangers of relying too much on oneself in the tightly interconnected world we live and work in today.

The limits of self-reliance

Self-reliance has tremendous advantages, which have been highlighted throughout this book. However, there are also drawbacks. Self-reliance should not be used to isolate oneself from other available strategies. In fact, the fourth and sixth domains of professionalism (*professional engagement* and *selflessness*) mandate engagement both inside and outside of your current setting.

We must also keep in mind that a Level III professional practices humility. Author Kingsley Amis captured this spirit when he said, "Self criticism must be my guide to action, and the first rule for its employment is that in itself it is not a virtue, only a procedure."[6] The procedure is only as good one's ability to execute it and willingness to follow it. The technology is only as good as the engineer, software designer, and the human who operates it. Systems have flaws. That is why at the end of the day, well trained professionals can step into these gaps and achieve good outcomes.

Deep professionalism training prepares anyone to analyze the strengths and weaknesses of all these related approaches as well as see the limits in themselves. This allows Level III professionals to design their own weapons for performance improvement, based upon their unique situation and environment.

---

[6] http://www.brainyquote.com/quotes/authors/k/kingsley_amis.html

Develop your own Area 51[7]

Area 51 is (allegedly) where the new weapons are designed, built, and tested for the United States Air Force. Originally, the famed *Lockheed Skunk Works* operations used the area to design, build, and test such forward-thinking projects as the Mach 3+ SR-71 *Blackbird* reconnaissance aircraft, thought by many to be decades ahead of its time. Similarly, Level III professionals can use this idea of developing new weapons in the battle for human performance. In the final analysis, the tools or strategies you choose to employ must be right for you.

> "In the real world, the battle for high performance (and against human error) is ultimately single warrior combat."

In the real world, the battle for high performance (and against human error) is ultimately single warrior combat. Although most of us operate in teams, sustaining high levels of performance demands individuals to be operating at or near their peaks across a vast domain of technical and nontechnical areas. That's a heck of a challenge.

Now it is on to our final chapter, where we take the new professionalism to the next organizational level.

---

[7] Area 51 was (some say still is) a secret military installation in southern Nevada and is also known as *Dreamland* and *Groom Lake*. The base's primary purpose is to support development and testing of experimental aircraft and weapons systems. The official government position that the USAF has an "operating location" near Groom Lake, but does not provide any further information.

> "Never underestimate the power of a few committed people to change the world. Indeed, it is the only thing that ever has."

Margaret Meade

Chapter 13

The Culture Connection: Building a Level III Organization

"Example is leadership."
Albert Schweitzer

"Authentic competence," he said, "that's what I'm looking for. We don't need any more show dogs that come in with great pedigrees but don't know how we do things here. We need huntin' dogs, but I can't find 'em anymore."

This conversation took place while interviewing a senior executive of a large international corporation on the topic of the new professionalism. He was lamenting the fact that his company was struggling to find quality talent as it expanded. As a result, he explained, his organization was becoming "more about PowerPoint briefings than production, sales and service."

Knowing very little about the talent pool in this gentleman's industry, but a little bit about hunting dogs, I took the conversation to the only place I could. "Well Sir," I asked. "If you

> "Even if organizations are able to establish a beachhead of Level III professionals inside their walls, these high achievers must be prepared to swim upstream inside established cultures."

can't find them, maybe you can get some pups with good noses and train them to hunt like you want?"

"We've done that, but they don't last in our culture. The old dogs around here seem to eat their young, or at least drive them away," he responded. "What is your culture like here?" I asked. He looked me straight in the eye and answered with complete honesty and a bit of remorse. "Honestly, I don't know anymore."

This senior executive felt lost about the state and direction of his organizational culture. I suspect he is not alone.

Organizational culture remains one of the most complex and studied issues in modern business and government. There are literally hundreds of studies, journal articles and books on the subject. It is not my intent to analyze or even review this vast expanse, but one thing is clear. Even if organizations are able to establish a beachhead of Level III professionals inside their walls, these high achievers must be prepared to swim upstream inside established cultures.

Does culture really trump all?

A short trip down the information highway courtesy of our friends (or overseers) at Google provides a taste of the current worldview on this question. After I typed in "culture trumps" and hit the search key, it took 0.06 seconds for 1,100,000 results to appear. A few of the highlights:

"Culture trumps strategy."

"Culture trumps policy."

"Culture trumps leadership."

"Culture trumps training."

"Culture trumps race."

"Culture trumps technology."

"Culture trumps everything."

Seriously? Culture trumps *everything*. That almost sounds like a Chuck Norris joke.[1] While I don't believe that culture is an all-powerful tsunami against which organizational leaders have no defense, there is little doubt that whatever it is – it is *powerful*. If Level III professionals are going to engage in new way inside their organizations, we better get a grip not only on what culture means, but also what we can do to influence it in a positive direction.

This brings us to the nebulous topic of *culture change*.

Traditional models of culture change

Culture change strategies are everywhere, nearly all espousing various methods that organizational leaders can use to shape the culture of their respective organizations. Most have merit. Some are exceptional. One of the most comprehensive and useful books I have on the topic is *Make it Glow*, by Tom DeCotis.[2] He ties in many of the aspects of the new professionalism, including ethics, human goodness, and the importance of personal and strategic leadership

---

[1] Being a huge Chuck Norris fan, I feel obligated to share my favorite CN joke. *What did they find when they shaved off Chuck Norris' beard? Another fist!*

[2] DeCotis, Tom. *Make it Glow: How to Build a Company reputation for Human Goodness, Flawless Execution and Being Best-in-Class*. Greenleaf Book Group Press. 2008.

in a single, actionable package for organizational leaders. If you are seeking information on the top down leadership angle of culture change, *Glow* is a great place to start.

But few culture change strategies talk about ways to change culture change from *below*, or from the *inside*. To be clear, it is not my intent to abandon the "culture change through leadership" model, but rather to complement it with an inside game of heightened professionalism.

Inside moves

In his seminal essay *Principles of War*, Prussian military strategist Carl von Clausewitz speaks of two critical needs for victory in battle. The first is *economy of effort*, which is simply the "judicious exploitation of manpower, materiel and time in relation to the achievement of objectives."[3]

In today's economic climate, a lean approach is a part of most smart business strategies. Clausewitz's second principle of relevance is the *concentration of force at a decisive point*,[4] meaning the application of resources at the point and time of greatest leverage. Unlike his contemporary Jomini[5] who espoused an "if-then" prescriptive approach, Clausewitz is adamant about preparing front line personnel to operate within the *friction and fog of war*. From his

---

[3] http://www.clausewitz.com/readings/Principles/index.htm
[4] http://www.clausewitz.com/readings/Principles/index.htm
[5] Antoine-Henri, baron Jomini (March 6, 1779 – March 24, 1869) was a general in the French and later in the Russian service, and one of the most celebrated writers on the Napoleonic art of war.

perspective, the fluidity of battle requires that the best decisions are made closest to the action by intelligent and experienced individuals on the front lines. The parallels for modern organizations are obvious.

The establishment of a cadre of Level III professionals leverages both Clausewitizian principles. It represents *economy of effort* through the relatively small number of trainees, as well as *concentration of force* by allowing this small group to focus on areas of greatest leverage as identified from <u>within</u> the organization by those closest to the battle.

In this manner, Level III's see problems and seize opportunities to improve the culture from the inside simultaneous and congruent with any top down initiatives. Their daily example of enhanced professional ethics, vocational excellence, continuous improvement, professional engagement, image, and selflessness creates *Level III cells of excellence* at multiple levels, rippling professionalism through the power of their example throughout the organization. In military jargon, these front line leaders exploit opportunities while operating inside the *commander's intent* – or vision and strategy of the leaders they work for.

To aid in the development of this inside game capacity, we have developed intense *Level III professionalism blitz* programs of 3-5 day duration for project and program leaders, management and executive teams to provide the background, metrics, tools and inspiration to develop and support the inside game of Level III professionals. These events are modeled after the proven *kaizen blitz* events that have been proven highly successful inside the quality movement.

These programs often work where other more traditional change efforts do not because the intensity and urgency of concentrated

"Truth be told, most culture change efforts are driven by one or more bad events in your organization's recent past. Why spend time, energy and money to study where you know longer want to be? Why expend resources to build data around a past or present you wish to leave behind?"

training overcomes the natural resistance to change. At these events, leaders and managers get the opportunity to assess their own professionalism, as well as that of the organization at large. Key areas of personal and organizational leverage are identified and then laser targeted with specific professionalism interventions. They leave with the expectation and initiative required to lead effectively and confidently within the fog and friction ever present in modern business and government.

Even armed with this type of training, the challenge of overcoming the inertia of the status quo is considerable, so leaders must establish the vision and desired outcomes of any change effort.

From here to where?

One of the most difficult questions that arise in any culture change initiative is *from what – to what*? Typically answering the first half of this question requires consultants armed with culture surveys and other instruments to come in and tell you what you probably already have a good feel for.

"*From what?*" is a tough question, but the current state of your organizational culture may be less relevant than you have been led to believe. Truth be told, most culture change efforts are driven by one or more bad events in your organization's recent past. Why spend time, energy and money to study where you know longer want to be? Why expend resources to build data around a past or present you wish to leave behind?

When resources are limited, (When *aren't* they?) you have a choice between studying your current situation or putting your time and energy into the change initiative. If you've already made the call for change and you've identified a path and desired end state, put your resources into the change effort. Employing Clausewitz's *economy of effort* principle allows organizational leaders to bypass concerns about the past and present and regain a future orientation.

A subtle shift to reduce resistance

Culture change announcements often result in the old guard grabbing their pitchforks and torches and chanting "kill the outlanders." So rather than packaging the effort as *culture change*, which probably mandates overcoming considerable resistance, consider undertaking the change initiative under the flag of *continuous improvement*.

Typically, continuous improvement is a standard part of most organizational structures and budgets. Senior executives will often have continuous improvement as a part of their formal job descriptions, and are more likely to support a less controversial approach.

This subtle shift in tactics allows leaders to budget and plan within existing structures to achieve culture change objectives. Additionally, continuous improvement efforts are much easier to place within the key functions that drive culture change, such as *selection, training,* and *evaluation* and when necessary, *remediation* for those not meeting standards. Let's take a brief look at each of these to see how promoting Level III professionalism within existing paradigms and functions can create the desired change with less disruption.

- *Selection.* All savvy human resource professionals know that it is far easier to select for attributes than to train them. By selecting for professionalism attributes that match your existing or desired culture, organizations can avoid the dilemma our VP was speaking about at the beginning of this chapter ("show dogs" who don't fit the culture). Hiring for pedigrees and specific vocational skill sets without matching to cultural norms creates a set of unknowns and could actually damage your culture.

    Internal selection for promotion or advancement is made much more predictable when you are able to assess the *professionalism* attributes of the candidates in advance. In small organizations, this is much easier though observation of the individual candidates over time. However, in large, geographically diverse organizations, this may not be possible. For this reason, we have created a set of assessment tools specifically to measure Level III professionalism attributes much in the same manner that current "personality profiles" are used by many HR departments.

    > "Level III professionalism training programs are designed to avoid this 'inverse outcome' trap by recognizing that you get one chance to make a first impression."

- *Training.* When you can't select for a desired attribute, you must train it. Training on-the-job professionals is expensive and often unpredictable. Taking working employees off the schedule and providing classroom or other training disrupts work schedules, and is often done in a casual "check the box" manner to comply with some existing of new training requirement. This sends the wrong message to employees who see these uninspired efforts as an indicator of management's commitment level to the change the training appears to advocate. Many culture change initiatives go off the rails quickly in this manner.

Level III professionalism training programs are designed to avoid this 'inverse outcome' trap by recognizing that you get one chance to make a first impression. The training is relevant, hard hitting and respects both the intellect and experience of adult learners.

- *Evaluation.* It is no secret that learning is enhanced when the adult learner knows that it is tied to his or her evaluation criteria. Level III programs make no apologies for this truth and build professionalism observation tools into quality assurance criteria and every supervisor's employee evaluation took kit. This takes some time and effort, but you get what you measure and adults learn better when they are held at risk for the training objectives.

Occasionally, even good employees fall of the track and require retraining or other remediation.

- *Remediation.* These are excellent opportunities to train Level III self-improvement skills contained in the *vocational excellence, continuous improvement,* and *professional engagement* domains. This avoids the impression and stigma often associated with those who perceive that they are being punished or retrained on how to do their jobs.

Embedding the new professionalism skill sets into existing program elements pave the way for the inside game to take shape and gain momentum.

Let's now take a quick look at how these small changes within existing structures can lead to significant organizational improvement.

Cultures form like crystals

Being a social scientist, I readily admit when I open a science book, I'm in a foreign land on dangerous ground. However, when a colleague pointed out the commonalities between how a crystal grows and the formation of cultures, it convinced me to risk the journey to the hard science section of my local library.

Crystals grow by a process called *nucleation* – which is the bonding of a few like-minded molecules in the center of an otherwise chaotic solution. Once there is a certain number of molecules joined, which is considered a *critical size*, the combined attractive forces of the *protocrystal* molecules become stronger. As this protocrystal floats around in solution, it encounters other molecules that feel the attractive force and join in, attaching themselves along the same patterns as the originals. That's how the crystal grows with predictable symmetry. The same holds true in the often chaotic solution we know as organizational culture.

> "When a group of Level IIIs are in the game, culture change occurs naturally and organically, like a force of nature."

A small core of high performing Level III professionals will attract others through the sheer force of example. It is important to note that a single molecule – or Level III – does not act in the same manner; it has not yet reached critical size, and will continue to fly solo in the solution until it can find a few like-minded friends. It is for this reason, the inculcation of the new professionalism into the core HR functions of *selection, training, evaluation* and *remediation* are so critical. They gradually build Level III competence through existing structures until critical size is reached.

Level III efforts gain momentum and traction when small groups of high performing professionals work closely together in the same division or on the same program or project.

When these conditions are met, there is no longer a need for "change agents," they merely go about their tasks operating at high levels and continuing to get better. No one has to "champion" a culture change from above, but it doesn't hurt to do so. When a group of Level IIIs are in the game, culture change occurs naturally and organically, like a force of nature.

Project teams are ideal places to start

Level III professionals are the seeds of culture change and project and program teams are ideal starting points. Most have short term objectives and enough visibility for synergies to develop and demonstrate the usefulness and competitive advantage of Level III performance to others over a short period of time.

Specifically tailored *Level III blitz* events are designed to prep small groups to fulfill this role in project and program teams. These 3-5 day concentrated programs provide the knowledge, tools and inspiration for a team of high achievers to begin a positive culture transformation. No one becomes a Level III professional overnight, but a jump start is a great way to kick off any effort.

In addition to the benefits provided through example, high performing professionalism has two other significant advantages.

Latent pathogens and latent potentials

One of the major outcomes of Level III performance is the ability for individuals closest to the action to root out underlying problems and seize opportunities in real time. This is what sociologist Ron Westrum calls a "culture of conscious inquiry," and is a key outcome of professionalism growth and empowerment. High performers with a Going Pro mindset are "fixers and finders" who lower risks and increase efficiencies within an organization as a matter of due course.

> "The core building block of a Level III professionalism culture is trust."

In 1990, Professor James Reason introduced the concept of *latent pathogens* to describe underlying issues that frequently combine into very negative outcomes under certain conditions. These unhealthy conditions lay dormant until activated by some external event or condition, and then *bang* – all hell breaks loose. Prior to the activation, these pathogens are present and often observable, but no action is taken to remove them because they haven't (yet) caused a negative outcome. They seem like insignificant issues, and unenlightened eyes and busy schedules allow them to fester.

The authors of *Resilience Engineering* suggest that

> Organizations that create alignment, awareness, and empowerment among their workforce are more likely to remove these latent pathogens from their environment and therefore reduce their pathogen load.[6]

In turn, this frees up resources for other critical tasks and systematically eradicates latent risks.

In addition to locating and remediating latent pathogens, a Level III professional will also activate *latent potentials* within themselves and coworkers. This is especially true for those "B players" who are looking for a means to contribute, but feel frustrated by stagnant advancement in jobs they feel overqualified for or by internal bureaucracies that don't make change easy, even when someone has a great idea.

"Because Level III professionals are accomplished in the domains or *professional ethics, vocational excellence,* and *professional engagement*, they require less oversight and are given more latitude for independent action. Confidence builds in both directions."

In this manner, the most significant and vital component of culture change is created – *trust*.

---

[6] Hollnagel, Erik. Woods, David, Leveson, Nancy. *Resilience engineering: concepts and precepts.* Ashgate. Aldershot UK. 2006.p. 63

How Level III professionalism promotes the "trust dividend"

The core building block of a Level III professionalism culture is trust. Stephen M. R. Covey explains why in his outstanding book, *The Speed of Trust: The One Thing That Changes Everything*.

> Low trust causes friction, whether it is caused by unethical behavior or by ethical but incompetent behavior (because even good intentions can never take the place of bad judgment). Low trust is the greatest cost in life and in organizations, including families. Low trust creates hidden agendas, politics, interpersonal conflict, interdepartmental rivalries, win-lose thinking, defensive and protective communication—all of which reduce the speed of trust. Low trust slows everything— every decision, every communication and every relationship.[7]

Put simply, decreased trust slows progress and increases costs.

Conversely, high levels of trust is a measurable accelerator and leads to less required oversight, fewer interruptions of workflow for "status reports" and significantly lower overhead in terms of oversight. Increased trust speeds progress and lowers cost.

There is little doubt that many modern organizations suffer from a lack of trust between management and the workforce. This is true in business and government, in large organizations and small. Because Level III professionals are accomplished in the domains or *professional ethics, vocational excellence,* and *professional engagement*, they require less oversight and are given more latitude for independent action.

---

[7] Covey, Stephen M. R. with Rebecca R. Merrill. *The Speed of Trust: the One Thing That Changes Everything.* Free Press, New York. 2006. Online at www.coveylink.com

Confidence builds in both directions.

Most significantly, these professionals typically operate within the workforce and their ethical excellence breeds trust both horizontally and vertically. Enhanced trust between management and the workforce is the inescapable outcome.

Trust breeds quality, efficiency and results. It also builds the culture of success that lifts all elements of the human capital assets currently in place. Employees feel more connected to their leadership, and executives sleep more soundly.

Increased trust is the most significant competitive advantage offered by Level III professionalism. In and of itself, it makes the effort worthwhile.

Human capital gains

At a conference a few years ago, I followed a well-respected human performance expert on stage and was faced with an uncomfortable moment. He had spent the previous 60 minutes telling the 1,500+ attendees that "all the easy things have been done" and in order to make any further inroads on profitability or safety, we "need to make significant investments to work the small margins we have not yet addressed." I tossed out my standard introduction and started by presentation by saying "With all due respect to our keynote speaker, I simply could not disagree more."

> "Increased trust is the most significant competitive advantage offered by Level III professionalism. In and of itself, it makes the effort worthwhile."

My point then – and now – is that we have not begun to leverage the full potential of people. I'm not talking about riding them harder or working them longer, but rather empowering them with new error control and opportunity seizing tools, providing a clear intent for them to drive improvement, and trusting them to do it.

Level III professionalism will change the dynamics in the board room as well as the assembly line. It has immediate applications for senior and middle management, program and project teams, first line supervisors, IT professionals, human resources, industrial safety, quality and continuous improvement programs, marketing, sales and customer service. Professionalism is for everyone.

How can one new concept or program impact all of these pieces of the puzzle? Heightened awareness seizes opportunities and reduces errors in all environments. By being able to see deeper into themselves and the situation, a new level of participatory excellence is not only possible, but practically guaranteed. Perhaps more than ever before in our history, people are making the difference between winning and losing. In our world of scarce resources, human capital is king.

Leadership creates the conditions for professional growth

Sir Edmund Hillary, the first European to scale Mount Everest, said it best. "It is not the mountain we conquer, but ourselves."[8] Professionalism, as newly defined, allows both formal and informal

---

[8] Found at http://thinkexist.com/quotation/it_is_not_the_mountain_we_conquer_but_ourselves/10675.html

leaders to rise within the constraints of existing resources.

Formal leaders are on the organizational chart. They have titles and offices with doors. They have incredible workloads. All too often this combination leads to ever increasing isolation.

Informal leaders can be anywhere in an organization. They might be in middle management, or sweeping the hallways on the night shift. They lead through example and the power of their personalities.

Level III professionalism can be – should be – the common ground. Recognized and appreciated by all who know the new standards, professionalism breeds respect and trust.

But it must be the formal leadership that creates the conditions for the culture shift towards greater professionalism to occur. Adoption of the new standards of professionalism is certainly a first step, but there is more that must be done. To illustrate this requirement I offer the last "war story" of the book.

Let me briefly set the scene of one of the most important leadership lessons I have ever learned.

In March of 1978, I was playing in the NCAA Division III men's basketball tournament for Albion College. We were in the quarterfinals and coached by a very young and inexperienced gentleman named Mike Turner. We were playing a very good team from Knoxville and were down by 12 points with 3:38 left in the game. We sensed defeat. I was on the bench, which was not all that unusual as I was a reserve guard and our top guys were on the floor.

Down by a dozen points with 3:38 left in the game, Coach Turner looked down the bench and called my name. Frankly, I wasn't sure he wasn't throwing in the towel and getting ready to empty the bench to let us all get some NCAA playoff minutes. That thought was quickly put to rest when Coach put his arm around me and said "This game is not over. We are about to hit a turning point. Don't let anybody quit. Keep us in the game until the momentum changes and then we win it down the stretch."

And that is exactly what happened.[9] We took the lead with 12 seconds left in the game and went on to the NCAA Final Four. As great as his words were, just as important is what Coach did not say. He didn't draw up a play on the grease board, he didn't tell us to play a tighter man-to-man defense, or to rebound better. He merely painted a positive outcome and turned us loose. *"This game is not over ... we are about to hit a turning point ... we win down the stretch."*

> "That is exactly what leaders can do to empower a sea change of professionalism when working with Level IIIs. Establish a positive vision of the future, express confidence, stay out of the tactics, and trust the team to execute."

With those simple words, he changed our mindset. We were no longer playing in fear of losing the final game of the season on our home court, instead we were participating in a thrilling come from behind victory. Nothing had changed on the floor, but everything changed in our minds. Coach Turner made the come from behind victory not only possible, but probable. He painted the future; the team bought in and played to the script.

That is exactly what leaders can do to empower a sea change of professionalism when working with Level IIIs. Establish a positive

---

[9] I'm not claiming to have personally turned the game around although I did hit the go ahead shot with 12 seconds left. (After missing a free throw that should have tied it a minute earlier.)

vision of the future, express confidence, stay out of the tactics, and trust the team to execute.

Final words

To borrow a phrase from Stephen Covey, "this book breathes hope." Hope for individuals who seek to achieve their potential; hope for organizations that are looking for a competitive edge; hope for resource-strapped executives trying to lead their companies to the next level, and hope for entire industries who are at risk of losing public confidence.

Professionalism is no longer a vague concept. It is a viable and achievable choice. In our highly competitive global marketplace, it has never been more critical. The path to Level III performance is not an easy one, but it is a predictable, viable and achievable alternative to the disease of sloppiness and apathy that has infected many of our professions. It is available to anyone and everyone with a will to improve with little more than the application of the principles contained here.

In the words of George Eliot, "it is never too late to be what you might have been."

Appendix A

Self-Assessment Scorecard

Add Subtotals from Chapter Assessments

_____ Professional Ethics (Chapter 6)

_____ Vocational Excellence (Chapter 7)

_____ Continuous Improvement (Chapter 8)

_____ Professional Engagement (Chapter 9)

_____ Professional Image (Chapter 10)

_____ Selflessness (Chapter 11)

TOTAL _____ (100 possible)

What now?

First, realize that there is no "pass-fail" grade on this assessment. A single data point does not define anything but where you perceive yourself at this moment in time. Keep this self-assessment confidential and begin to reflect and work upon all six domains with the tools provided in the accompanying GoingPro *Roadblocks, On Ramps,* and *Fast Lanes* professionalism development tools at the end of chapters 6-11.

Appendix B
Going Pro Assessments and Training Products

Assessments

GoingPro Quickstart Toolkit™

The *Quickstart Toolkit* is a 30-page professionalism self-assessment and personal inventory designed as an introduction to Level III professionalism. Its purpose is to heighten personal awareness across all six domains of professionalism and provide actionable tools for immediate application in the workplace. It includes immediate action steps, and concludes with a *Personal Professionalism Improvement Plan* complete with specific next steps and a timeline to drive immediate improvement. Perfect for workshops and self-improvement efforts. Available through convergentperformance.com.

Professional Attributes Strength Inventory™ (PASI)

The *Professional Attributes Strength Inventory* is an in-depth assessment designed by organizational psychologists at Corvirtus, LLC, a company that specializes in reliable psychometric instruments for multiple industries. The PASI assesses multiple aspects of personal perceptions and professionalism values to create a personalized professionalism profile. This instrument is available in a text version or online, and participants receive a detailed and confidential personalized report via email with their results and recommendations for next step improvements within days after completion. Available through corvirtus.com.

GoingPro Chronos™

GoingPro Chronos is a powerful tool that allows individuals to track and leverage trends in their professional development over a prolonged period (5 and 10 year subscriptions). As an extension of the *Professional Attributes Strength Inventory, Chronos* continuously updates progress on all six professionalism domains allowing individuals to pursue a growth-based strategy based upon the deliberate practice model. This instrument is ideal for those who are in it for the long haul and understand the value of continuous, objective feedback to their professional development. Available through corvirtus.com.

GoingPro 360™

GoingPro 360 is also provided by Corvirtus and takes the next step in professionalism assessment with a tool that utilizes multi-rater feedback provided by subordinates, peers, supervisors, and if desired, customers. It is ideal for personal feedback or for selection of personnel for instructor, mentor, or supervisory positions where a high level of professionalism is critical. Feedback is provided by secure email to ensure confidentiality. Available through corvirtus.com.

Training Tools and Programs

Going Pro and Blue Threat books available at corporate rates for orders over 25 through pygmybooks.com

GoingPro Team Study Guides

Team study guides are available for those who wish to use *Going Pro* as a training tool in small groups. It provides chapter-by-chapter applications, discussion notes, and probing questions to allow each team member to customize the content of the book to their own organization and environment. The study guide enables systemic culture change by creating cadres of Level III professionals within your organization. Also available through pygmybooks.com.

GoingPro Facilitator Training and Instructor Packages

Going Pro facilitator training is provided exclusively by Convergent Performance, a veteran-owned small business that specializes in optimizing human performance in all settings. The three-day intensive program includes deep instruction in the six domains of professionalism as well as a full package of resources (case studies, PowerPoint presentations, videos, assessments, instructor guide) to allow new facilitators "turn-key" success inside their own organizations. Certified facilitators are provided discounts on all GoingPro products and assessments for use in their organization. These programs are held at various locations around the globe or can be coordinated for your location with advanced scheduling. Available through convergentperformance.com.

Blue Threat Proverbs™ Poster Pack. Thirty full color posters of the "Blue Threat Proverbs" provide motivation and daily reminders of key aspects of personal accountability, error control, and Level

III professionalism attributes. Available in various sizes through convergentperformance.com.

GoingPro Workshops

Four levels of GoingPro workshops provide end-to-end training in Level III professionalism. All workshops are delivered by highly trained Convergent facilitators. Introduction and Advanced workshops are also delivered online via live and recorded webinars. All workshops available through convergentperformance.com.

- **Introduction to Level III professionalism.** This ½ day workshop (or three-hour webinar) introduces the concept of three levels of professionalism, deliberate practice and the six domains of the new professionalism and is ideal for all levels of your workforce. It utilizes the *GoingPro Quickstart*™ toolkit and concludes with the development of a personal professionalism improvement plan for each participant. Discount pricing on *Going Pro* books and Team Study Guides are available in conjunction with this workshop.

- **Advanced professionalism workshop.** This ½ day workshop (or three-hour webinar) is tailored for managers (or prospective managers), instructors, evaluators, safety and quality assurance personnel, as well as others in position of oversight and authority. In addition to the fundamentals of the new professionalism, the program utilizes the Professional Attributes Strength Inventory to provide deep insights into personal levels of professionalism. The program capstone is a set of skills and tools for support and advocacy for culture improvement and internal Level III professional development. *Introduction to Level III professionalism* workshop is recommended, but not required for participation in this program. Same day scheduling for back-to-back workshops available. Discount pricing on GoingPro books and Team Study Guides are available in conjunction with this workshop.

- **Level III professionalism blitz events.** Level III blitz events are designed to jump start management, program and project teams in all aspects of professional excellence. First round blitz events take place over three days and provide the background, metrics, tools, and inspiration to develop and support the inside game of Level III professionals. These events are modeled after the proven *kaizen blitz* events that have been proven highly successful inside the quality movement. Blitz events often work where other more traditional change efforts do not because the intensity and urgency of concentrated training overcomes the natural resistance to change. At these events, leaders and managers get the opportunity to assess their own professionalism, as well as that of the organization at large. Key areas of personal and organizational leverage are identified and then laser targeted with specific professionalism interventions. They leave with the expectation and initiative required to lead effectively and confidently within the fog and friction ever present in modern business and government.

- **GoingPro executive retreats.** Level III executive retreats are designed for senior executives and conducted in settings conducive to learning, reflection and planning. The ability to get away from the daily grind and focus on enhancing professionalism are crucial to maintaining a positive workforce and getting people excited about the possibilities of activating "latent potentials" to achieve your vision and strategy. Retreats can be customized to the needs of your organization or provided "turn key" with Level III mentors guiding your team toward specific goals and objectives to optimize your human capital and permanently establish a culture of Level III professionalism inside your organization. Good conversation, fine cigars and reasonably good wine come with the package. Programs are limited to 12 attendees.

- **GoingPro Professional Mentor Certification Program™.** Mentorship of professionalism is far more than finding an experienced person with a good track record and asking them to pass along the party line. This formal certification program provides two-way professionalism survey instruments, personal professionalism inventories, structured improvement plans, and interpreted case studies, all designed to enable the mentor to get their mentorship project off to a flying start. Four-day intensive programs train and certify new mentors in the art and science of Level III professionalism, as well as the core skills of mentorship.

Selected Bibliography and Resources

Anderson Lydia E. and Sandra B. Bolt. Professionalism: Skills for Workplace Success (2nd Edition). Prentice Hall. 2010.

Barber, Safdar, and Franklin. "Can human error theory explain non-adherence?" Pharmacy World and Science (2005): 300-304.

Colvin, Geoff. Talent is Overrated. Portfolio. 2008.

Covey, Stephen M. R. with Rebecca Merrill. The Speed of Trust: The One Thing That Changes Everything. Free Press. 2006.

Csikszentmihalyi, Mihalyi, and Isabella Selega Csikszentmihalyi. Optimal Experience: Psychological Studies of Flow in Consciousness. Cambridge University Press, 1988.

Csizkszentmihalyi, Mihaly. Flow: The Psychology of Optimal Experience. Harper Perennial, 1990.

Damasio, Antonio R. Descartes' Error. Quill, 1994.

Dekker, Sidney. The Field Guide to Understanding Human Error. Ashgate, 2006.

Dekker, Sidney. Just Culture: Balancing Safety and Accountability. Ashgate, 2008.

DeCotis, Tom. Make it Glow: How to Build a Company Reputation for Human Goodness, Flawless Execution, and Being Best-In-Class. Greenleaf Book Group Press, 2008.

Dismukes, Berman, and Loukopoulos. The Limits of Expertise: Rethinking Pilot Error and the Causes of Airline Accidents. Ashgate, 2007.

Dörner, Dietrich. The Logic of Failure: Recognizing and Avoiding Error in Complex Situations. Perseus Books, 1996.

Ericsson, Charness, Feltovich, and Hoffman. The Cambridge Handbook of Expertise and Expert Performance. Cambridge University Press, 2006.

Ericsson, Prietula, and Cokely. "The Making of an Expert." Harvard Business Review (July-Aug. 2007): 115-121.

Freidson, Eliot. Professionalism, the Third Logic: On the Practice of Knowledge. University of Chicago Press, 2001.

Gardner, Howard. Frames of Mind: The Theory of Multiple Intelligences. Basic Books. 1983

Gawande, Atul. Better: A Surgeon's Notes on Performance. Metropolitan Books, 2007.

Gladwell, Malcolm. Outliers: The Story of Success. Little, Brown and Company, 2008.

Gohm, Baumann, and Sniezek. "Personality in Extreme Situations." Journal of Research in Personality (Sept. 2001): 388-399.

Gonzales, Laurence. Deep Survival: Who Lives, Who Dies and Why. Norton, 2003.

Groopman, Jerome. How Doctors Think. Houghton Mifflin, 2007.

Halberstam, David. The Reckoning. Morrow, 1986.

Hallinan, Joseph T. Why We Make Mistakes: How We Look Without Seeing, Forget Things in Seconds, and Are All Pretty Sure We Are Way above Average. Broadway Books, 2009.

Heath, Chip and Dan Heath. Switch: How to Change Things When Change is Hard. Broadway Books, 2010.

Huntsman, Jon. Winners Never Cheat: Even in Difficult Times. Wharton School Publishing, 2009.

Kidder, Rushworth M. How Good People Make Tough Choices: Resolving the Dilemmas of Ethical Living. Simon and Schuster, 1995.

Kern, Tony. Flight Discipline. McGraw-Hill, 1996.

Kern, Tony. Blue Threat: Why to Err is Inhuman. Colorado Springs, Pygmy Books, 2009.

Klein, Gary. Intuition at Work: Why Developing Your Gut Instincts Will Make You Better at What You Do. Currency, 2002.

Klein, Gary. Sources of Power: How People Make Decisions. The MIT Press, 1999.

Koch, Charles. The Science of Success: How Market-Based Management Built the World's Largest Private Company. Wiley, 2007.

Krause, Eliot A. Death of the Guilds: Professions, States, and the Advance of Capitalism. Yale University Press, 1996.

Kultgen, John H. Ethics and Professionalism. University of Pennsylvania Press, 1988.

Lagadec, P., Phelps, J. Preventing Chaos in a Crisis: Strategies for Prevention, Control and Damage Limitation. McGraw Hill, 1991.

Maister, David H. True Professionalism: The Courage to Care About Your People, Your Clients, and Your Career. Free Press, 2000.

McDonough, W., Braungart, M. Cradle to Cradle: Remaking the Way We Make Things. North Point Press, 2002.

Moore, Thomas. Care of the Soul: A Guide for Cultivating Depth and Sacredness in Everyday Life. Harper Perennial, 1992.

Nickerson, Raymond S. "Confirmation Bias: A Ubiquitous Phenomenon in Many Guises." Review of General Psychology (1998): 175-220.

Pinker, Steven. How the Mind Works. Norton, 1997.

Polyani, Michael. Personal Knowledge: Towards a Post-Critical Philosophy. University of Chicago Press, 1958.

Polyani, Michael and Amartya Sen. The Tacit Dimension. University of Chicago Press, 2009.

Reason, James. Human Error. New York: Cambridge University Press, 1990.

Reason, James. Managing the Risks of Organizational Accidents. Ashgate, 1997.

Ross, Phillip E. "The Expert Mind." Scientific American (Aug. 2006): 64-71.

Senge, Peter M. The Fifth Discipline: The Art and Science of The Learning Organization. Currency Doubleday, 1990.

Simon, Herbert A. Administrative Behavior. Free Press, 1997.

Smith, Perry M. Taking Charge. National Defense University Press, 1986.

Sullivan, William M. Work and Integrity: The Crisis and Promise of Professionalism in America. Jossey-Bass/Carnegie Foundation for the Advancement of Teaching, 2004.

Taleb, Nicholas Nassim. The Black Swan: The Impact of the Highly Improbable. Random House, 2007.

Vaughan, Diane. "The Dark Side of Organizations: Mistake, Misconduct, and Disaster." The Annual Review of Sociology (1999): 271-305.

Waddle, Scott. The Right Thing. Integrity Publishers, 2002.

Weick, Karl E., and Sutcliffe, Kathleen M. Managing the Unexpected: Assuring High Performance in an Age of Complexity, Jossey Bass. 2001.

White, Jerry. Honesty, Morality & Conscience. NavPress, 1979.

Wiersma, Bill and Tony La Russa. The Power of Professionalism: The Seven Mind-Sets that Drive Performance and Build Trust. Ravel Media, 2011.

Index

Symbols

10,000 hour rule 106, 108, 109

A

accountability 8, 71, 77, 142, 146, 147, 266, 315
air traffic controllers 23
Al Haynes 286
apathy 2, 13, 17, 99, 311
arrogance 228
assessment 4, 15, 73, 84, 85, 86, 88, 91, 92, 93, 94, 95, 97, 100, 118, 140, 156, 157, 192, 193, 215, 238, 239, 266, 300, 312, 313, 314
Atlanta Public Schools 14, 129, 130, 133
attentive listening 249, 255, 256
authenticity 227, 228, 229, 244
authority gradient 76, 285
automation airmanship 278

B

bar association 57
behavior-based safety 282
benchmarking 118, 213
Beverly Hall 130
blue threat iii, iv, 3, 7, 8, 10, 11, 64, 70, 94, 95, 108, 117, 120, 134, 154, 156, 175, 176, 177, 178, 182, 184, 185, 186, 193, 271, 287, 315, 321, 330
blue threat report and analysis tool 117, 185

C

calibration 185
Carl von Clausewitz 296
cheating 14, 129, 130, 132, 133, 134, 135, 136, 138
civility 207, 211
clergy 23
commander's intent 297
compliance iii, 49, 51, 68, 69, 70, 152, 154, 156, 160, 161, 165, 260, 284
concentration of force 296, 297
confidentiality 264, 314
confirmation bias 88, 190, 228
conscience 139
constructive feedback 63, 159, 217
continuous improvement 4, 11, 87, 99, 154, 158, 170, 175, 176, 178, 181, 185, 186, 193, 194, 241, 263, 297, 299, 300, 301, 308
corrosive narcissism 137
Corvirtus 140
crew resource management 285
crystal model 16
culture iii, vi, 9, 10, 16, 17, 26, 27, 28, 33, 34, 67, 86, 96, 125, 126, 131, 133, 134, 137, 195, 240, 263, 264, 291, 294, 295, 296, 297, 298, 299, 300, 301, 302, 303, 304, 305, 306, 307, 309, 315, 316, 318, 319
culture change 9, 10, 16, 86, 295, 296, 298, 299, 300, 301, 302, 303, 305, 315
culture of conscious inquiry 304
customer service 15, 202, 204, 205, 206, 207, 210, 219, 220, 308
cynicism 2

D

deliberate practice 2, 14, 83, 98, 103, 107, 108, 110, 111, 113, 116, 118, 119, 175, 177, 179, 180, 209, 215, 218, 251, 256, 263, 314, 316
Dietrich Dörner 27
domains of professionalism 3, 4, 5, 14, 98, 259, 271, 288, 313, 315

E

economy of effort 296, 297, 299
Edward Deming 76, 81, 89, 285
electronic etiquette 237
elitism 66
esprit d'corps 211

F

facebook 200, 230, 231, 232, 233, 235
fifth discipline 279
flow 48, 49, 59, 112, 113, 114, 115, 188, 233, 251
fog of war 296

G

generations in aviation 265
Geoff Colvin 102, 107
Gideons Elementary School 131
going pro 8
going pro chronos 93, 140, 314
golden parachute 22
growth-based professionalism 14
guilds 44, 45, 46, 47, 48, 49, 58, 71

H

Heather Vogell 129, 130
Herbert William Heinrich 281
history of professionalism v, 13
honesty 71, 92, 127, 133, 135, 139, 142, 143, 144, 294
human error 8
human reliability 282, 283
humility 33, 228, 249, 250, 251, 252, 253, 256, 263, 269, 270, 271, 288

I

impression management 228
incompetence 56, 140, 228
industry best practices 220

innovation 47, 51, 182, 183, 184, 275, 285
integration 15, 183, 184, 185
integrity 54, 66, 70, 133, 135, 139, 142, 144, 228
international organization for standardization (ISO) 52
intrapersonal intelligence 249, 253, 271

J

James Reason 280, 304
J.D. Powers and Associates 86
John Donne 199, 201, 217
John F. Kennedy 77
Jon Huntsman 136
Josephson Institute of Ethics 135

K

kaizen 185, 195, 297, 317
K. Anders Ericsson 103, 105, 106, 116

L

laissez faire professionalism 13
latent pathogens 304, 305
latent potentials 304, 305, 317
level III cells of excellence 297
level III organization vi, 16
level III professionalism blitz 297, 317
level III professionals 5, 10, 108, 119, 138, 165, 168, 203, 204, 206, 220, 229, 237, 238, 251, 268, 280, 281, 283, 284, 285, 288, 289, 293, 294, 295, 297, 302, 303, 305, 306, 315, 317
level II professionals 4
level II pros 4, 70
level I professionalism 68
level I professionals 4, 69, 83, 260
limits of data use 88
linkedIn 230
locus of control 175
loyalty 55, 133, 142, 145
loyalty vs. honesty 127

M

Malcolm Gladwell 106, 108
Mark Twain 138
mediocrity 65, 155
mentor 94, 117, 144, 159, 191, 211, 218, 243, 254, 257, 258, 259, 260, 261, 262, 264, 265, 266, 269, 314, 318
mentoring 249, 254, 256, 257, 271
Merlin Effect 271
Mihaly Csikszenmihalyi 112
mySpace 230
myth of compliance 70, 135

N

narcissism 137, 267
national transportation safety board viii, 3, 61, 63
negative feedback 88, 190, 192
negative force multipliers 26
networking 214, 229, 231, 238
normalization of deviance 69, 70
normalization of excellence 120

O

outsourced ethics 128

P

paired professional 262, 263, 264
personal feedback 9, 314
personal improvement 9, 159, 180, 193, 200, 267
Peter Senge 77, 279
pilots iii, iv, 23, 54, 56, 64, 202, 277
police 23, 235
police officers 23
politicians 23
primary-backup inversion 276
probabilistic risk analysis 283
proceduralization 281, 282, 283
professional attributes strength inventory 93, 140, 313, 314, 316

professional engagement 4, 11, 99, 186, 195, 200, 201, 209, 213, 215, 216, 285, 288, 297, 301, 305, 306
professional ethics 4, 11, 33, 92, 99, 120, 125, 126, 128, 134, 140, 142, 144, 145, 146, 147, 170, 228, 284, 297, 305, 306
professional image 4, 73, 99, 221, 225, 226, 227, 228, 229, 235, 236, 238, 242, 243
professionalism behaviors 3
professionalism best practice 86
professionalist 5, 13, 71, 72
professional standards 3, 27, 28, 53, 56, 57, 73, 112, 152

Q

quality assurance 22, 46, 133, 283, 301, 316

R

redefining airmanship iii, 183, 330
ripple effect 10
Robert Sumwalt viii, 61, 63
rule of law 133

S

safety management systems 279
satchel paige 75
self-esteem 29, 63, 64, 68, 88, 126, 137, 230
self-importance 228
selflessness vii, 4, 15, 99, 211, 228, 244, 251, 253, 259, 266, 271, 288, 297
self-reliance 288
servant leadership 251, 252, 253, 254
Sheilagh Ogilvie 47
situational ethics 14, 128, 134
social networking 229, 231
surgeons 22
"Swiss Cheese" 165, 280
"Swiss Cheese" model 280
systems thinking 77, 279

T

Ted Williams 139
Telemon of Arcadia 182
the fifth discipline 77, 279, 323
Tom DeCotis 295
Tommy Tutone 75
trust 23, 58, 59, 81, 85, 88, 89, 90, 125, 232, 258, 260, 304, 305, 306, 307, 309, 310, 311

U

unethical conduct 133
united flight 232 286
united states marine 3
united states marine corps 3
untapped professionalism 26
untrustworthiness 228

V

vocational excellence 4, 99, 147, 151, 152, 154, 157, 158, 160, 163, 167, 170, 212, 228, 284, 297, 301, 305, 306

About the Author

Dr. Tony Kern is the CEO of Convergent Performance; a veteran-owned small business dedicated to optimizing human performance and reducing human error in high risk environments. Tony is one of the world's leading authorities on human performance and the author of six previous books on the subject, including *Redefining Airmanship, Flight Discipline*, and *Blue Threat: Why to Err is Inhuman*. Tony has deep operational and leadership experience as a Command Pilot and Flight Examiner in the B-1B bomber, as well as service as the Chair of the Air Force Human Factors Steering Group and Director and Professor of Military History at the USAF Academy. Upon retirement from the Air Force, Dr. Kern served as the National Aviation Director for the U.S. Forest Service, where he directed the largest non-military government aviation program in the world in support of federal wildland fire suppression. He has appeared frequently on talk radio and TV and has received multiple awards for his work, including the USAF Academy McDermott Award for Research Excellence (1999), Flight Safety Foundation Distinguished Service Award (2003) for Aviation Leadership and the Aviation Week and Space Technology Laurel Award (2002) for Outstanding Achievement in Government and Military Aviation. Tony holds Masters Degrees in Public Administration and Military History as well as the Doctorate in Higher Education from Texas Tech, specializing in human factors training design. He is a rabid Air Force Falcons and Detroit Red Wings fan and enjoys outdoor sports of all kinds. He and his wife Shari split their time between their home in Monument, Colorado, and their "Fortress of Solitude" at an undisclosed location high in the Rocky Mountains.